Stylized

A SLIGHTLY OBSESSIVE HISTORY OF
STRUNK & WHITE'S *THE ELEMENTS OF STYLE*

MARK GARVEY

A Touchstone Book
PUBLISHED BY SIMON & SCHUSTER

NEW YORK   LONDON   TORONTO   SYDNEY

Touchstone
A Division of Simon & Schuster, Inc.
1230 Avenue of the Americas
New York, NY 10020

First Touchstone hardcover edition October 2009

TOUCHSTONE and colophon are
registered trademarks of Simon & Schuster, Inc.

For information about special discounts for bulk purchases,
please contact Simon & Schuster Special Sales at
1-866-506-1949 or business@simonandschuster.com.

The Simon & Schuster Speakers Bureau can bring authors
to your live event. For more information or to book an event
contact the Simon & Schuster Speakers Bureau at 866-248-3049
or visit our website at www.simonspeakers.com.

Designed by Ruth Lee-Mui

Manufactured in the United States of America

1 3 5 7 9 10 8 6 4 2

Library of Congress Cataloging-in-Publication Data

Garvey, Mark.
Stylized : a slightly obsessive history of Strunk & White's
Elements of Style / by Mark Garvey.
p.   cm.
1. Strunk, William, 1869–1946. Elements of style.   2. Authorship—Style manuals.
3. English language—Rhetoric.   4. English language—Style.   I. Title.
PE1408.S7724   2009
808'042—dc22   2009007166

ISBN 978-1-4165-9092-7
ISBN 978-1-4391-6063-3 (eBook)

For Deb, Sam, and Sarah

The greatest thing a human soul ever does in this world is to see something and tell what it saw in a plain way. . . . To see clearly is poetry, prophecy, and religion all in one.

—JOHN RUSKIN

Oh! Blessed rage for order . . .

—WALLACE STEVENS

CONTENTS

INTRODUCTION

Credo

I hate the guts of English grammar.
—E. B. WHITE

Cards on the table: I love *The Elements of Style.* I love the idea of it; I love its execution. I love the book's history, and I love its attitude. I love the fact that it makes some people nuts. I love its trim size. I love the trade dress of the 1979 third edition: The authors' last names fill the top half of the honey-mustard cover in a stocky, crimson, sans serif typeface—as late seventies as Huggy Bear's hat—with the title itself rendered in thinner, mostly serifed type, black, in the bottom half. And in the bottom right corner, reversed out white inside a black triangle is this come-on: "With Index." Nice.

Over the years, I have collected multiple copies of *The Elements of Style,* though without much in the way of method or even, really, intent. I am apparently unable to pass up nicely preserved editions in used-book stores; it's the same sort of trouble some people face when confronted with a heretofore unseen edition of Wallace Stevens's *Harmonium* or a cache of Wodehouse novels—or, for others, an unopened six-pack of Billy beer. The copy of *Elements* in my house that has seen the most action is a paperback third edition from my college years. Its yellowed pages are edged with my own marginalia, scribbled in the heat of new revelation, no doubt, but so old and so sloppily written that it's mostly indecipherable now.

My rarest copy is a 1959 first edition, first printing, in great condition, including a perfectly intact dust jacket (thin, elegant black and white serifed type over a background color that a kitchen-appliance manufacturer might call Harvest Gold), that I found on a cold afternoon's romp through Bookmans Used Books in Flagstaff, Arizona. I paid four dollars for it, an edition that I have seen marked as high as two hundred dollars elsewhere in the used-book trade.

My favorite copy, however, is from the fourteenth printing of the 1979 edition. The book is case-bound, with a vinyl-impregnated buckram cover, forest green. Its signatures are Smyth-sewn; its dust jacket is flawless, in the ochre-red-black design just described, and protected by a Mylar cover. It is a pristine edition in all respects but one: A previous owner, perhaps fighting sleep in a mid-April English class—windows open, dogwoods in the school yard blinding white in the afternoon light, fat bees at work among the blooms—etched his name in red block letters across the top edge of the book's pages: PERKINS.

Perkins! Are we keeping you up? Sit up straight, man, and contemplate the prize you hold in your hand. Few books of this size (thin as a buttermilk pancake, six ounces waterlogged), in fact, few books of any size, have had the impact on American literary culture and thought that *The Elements of Style* has. Ounce for ounce, it has done more to establish an American ideal of good prose style than any other book or any teacher, living or dead. Its authors, William Strunk Jr. and E. B. (Elwyn Brooks) White, have joined the pantheon of twentieth-century creative duos whose names, over time, have been transformed into brands, if not movements. Think Rodgers and Hammerstein, the Wright brothers, Tracy and Hepburn, Lennon-McCartney. In fact, *The Elements of Style* is often called "Strunk and White," usually run together in the pronunciation, "strunkenwhite," the authors' names forever fused, as in "Perkins, please revisit strunkenwhite, Rule 12." And, as with most great duos, the names themselves are now powerful enough to conjure by. For generations the book, by its title or its authors' names, has been widely venerated as a sure, succinct guide to the fundamentals of good writing. But there's more to it than that. No simple book of tips about clear writing sells in the kinds of numbers this book sells. There's something else going on.

The Elements of Style as we know it today almost didn't happen. It took a fat slice of chance circumstance, and thirty-eight years, to draw the elements together. William Strunk Jr., a professor of English at Cornell University, in Ithaca, New York, self-published the first edition of the book in 1918. I have held a copy in the Cornell archives; it's a slight thing, only forty-three pages, with a lightly textured card-stock cover. Intended as a quick-reference guide for his students, *The Elements of Style* covered the basics of clear and clean writing—tips on usage, composition, word choice, spelling—and it simplified Strunk's task of grading papers and saved him the cost, in both time and tedium, of using valuable class time to reiterate the fundamentals. The book's advice was useful and accurate, it covered only the essentials, and its tone was brisk. Strunk's *Elements of Style* sold in the campus bookstore for twenty-five cents, and it enjoyed a respectable run at Cornell, going through several editions in Strunk's lifetime. One of the Cornellians plunking down his quarter in 1919 was E. B. White, a student in Strunk's English Usage and Style class.

There were plenty of things about college young Elwyn didn't care for, but the future essayist, children's author, and voice of *The New Yorker* magazine liked this class, and he liked William Strunk. After White's graduation in 1921, he and Strunk remained friends, but White's memory of *The Elements of Style* eventually faded.

Time passed. Lots of it. E. B. White began his long career at *The New Yorker* in 1926. The Depression came and went. Collections of White's essays, sketches, and poems were published. World War II rolled through. White wrote and published his first book for children, *Stuart Little*. William Strunk Jr., after a forty-six-year teaching career and nine years of retirement, passed away. White published the children's classic *Charlotte's Web* and still more collected essays. Finally, in the spring of 1957, thirty-eight years after he had last laid eyes on the book, and eleven years after Strunk's death, White received a copy of the 1918 edition of *The Elements of Style* in the mail; it had been sent by an old college friend who thought White would find it amusing. What happened next is well known to *Elements* fans—it's recounted in the introduction of every edition—and it's where the story really begins.

When Paul McCartney met John Lennon, at a Quarry Men gig in Liverpool, his first impulse was to pick up a guitar and play. When White re-met *The Elements of Style* in 1957, he, too, turned to his art: He took to the typewriter to tell his readers about *Elements* and about William Strunk. In a "Letter from the East" column published that summer in *The New Yorker*, E. B. White wrote about the "rich deposits of gold" he had rediscovered in the little book and about its author, whom he recalled as friendly, funny, audacious, and self-confident. "Will knew where he stood," White wrote. "He scorned the vague, the tame, the colorless, the irresolute. He felt it was worse to be irresolute than to be wrong." Strunk tickled White, and White admired his old professor's outlook: Say what you mean, and say it clearly.

The "Letter from the East" caught the eye of Jack Case, a *New Yorker* reader and alert editor working in the college book department of The Macmillan Company. Immediately after reading White's tribute to Strunk, maybe even before finishing it, Case contacted White to say that his company was interested in publishing *The Elements of Style* and using White's essay as the book's introduction. They struck an agreement, and, over the next year, White performed a thorough overhaul and updating of Strunk's original text; revised his *New Yorker* essay to work as the book's introduction; wrote a foreword, "A Note on This Book"; and added a new final chapter, "An Approach to Style." The result, a collaborative teacher-student effort that spanned four decades (not to mention the great divide), was Strunk and White's *The Elements of Style*. First published in 1959, the book vaulted the charts like "Love Me Do" and has hovered in the ether ever since. Before White's death in 1985, two more editions were published, in 1972 and 1979. The current edition, the fourth, was published in 1999.

We've already seen that my tender feelings for *The Elements of Style* extend even to the physical book itself. I recognize that's a little peculiar. In my defense, I'm not the first bibliophile guilty of cherishing a book nearly as much for its look and its feel in the hand as for its content. And, as I think about it, this appreciation for a book's shape and structure over, or aside from, its subject matter is an apt parallel to the main argument of *The Elements of Style* itself—the idea that a clear conception of *form,* the mechanics of communicating ideas through writing, stands behind and makes possible the successful expression of intellectual *content.* The Strunk and White prescription, distilled, is this: Master the fundamentals of good form, and, assuming you have something to say, the results—communication, style, *art*—will take care of themselves.

Elements enthusiasts are in large supply—the book has sold well over 10 million copies since 1959—and they tend to voice their praise with Strunkian directness. "Most books about writing are filled with bullshit," says Stephen King in his best-selling *On Writing: A Memoir of the Craft.* "One notable exception is *The Elements of Style.* There is little or no detectable bullshit in that book. Every aspiring writer should read *The Elements of Style.*" Strunk and White sit firmly in the top quarter of the Modern Library's list of 100 Best Nonfiction books. *The Elements of Style* is quoted and recommended warmly in scores of other guides to writing, from William Zinsser's *On Writing Well* and *The Associated Press Stylebook* to *Barron's How to Prepare for the New SAT.*

Today, in the bookstore on the Cornell campus, students can choose from five varieties of *Elements*: a paperback or hardcover fourth edition, a reprint of Strunk's 1918 original or his 1920 revision, and a popular 2005 version of the fourth edition illustrated by the artist and designer Maira Kalman. It is also available in other media. An audio edition, read by *Angela's Ashes* author Frank McCourt, was released in 2008. (McCourt, interviewed for this book, expressed surprise that he had been chosen for the narration job: "It's beyond me—they could've gotten someone with a voice like George Plimpton's, a Harvard kind of voice." But it turns out McCourt's musical accent is a perfect accompaniment to the playful and precise rhythms of Strunk and White.) There is even a video version, created in the late eighties, based on the third edition and hosted by the bow-tied commentator Charles Osgood. For *Elements* or Osgood completists, copies are still obtainable online. Occasionally the book jumps genres entirely: In 1981, a short ballet based on *The Elements of Style* was staged in New York by the choreographer Matthew

Nash. ("The dancers were merry," the *Times* reviewer offered, "but Mr. Nash never quite decided what he wanted his ballet to be. . . . And, surely, neither Mr. Strunk nor Mr. White would have approved of indecisiveness.") And in 2005, in conjunction with the publication of Maira Kalman's illustrated edition of *Elements,* an operatic song cycle composed by Nico Muhly, *The Elements of Style: Nine Songs,* was performed in the reading room of the New York Public Library before a sold-out audience. The tenor and soprano were accompanied by viola, banjo, and percussion (including vibraphone, teacups, typewriter, and duck call). *Newsweek*'s reviewer was unsure: "Unfortunately, the operatic style of the piece rendered the lyrics all but unintelligible to this listener—in ironic contrast to the simplifying ethos of 'Elements'—though that may be more the fault of the acoustics of the library venue, which was, after all, designed for silence."

For decades, other publishers, on seeing the eye-popping sales of *The Elements of Style,* have whistled quietly through their teeth and then set out to replicate its success (or at least test the drafting effect of trailing in its wake) by appending the phrase "The Elements of" to titles on a Dummies-rivaling array of subjects. There are books on "The Elements of" graphic design, legal writing, architecture, computer programming, drawing, mentoring, boatbuilding, information theory, horse training, public speaking, editing, politics, art, music, health, organic gardening, golf, bankruptcy, ethics, prayer, and more. Most of those other publishers have eventually discovered that the title is not where the magic lives.

While strong in its chapter-to-chapter specifics and as useful as a pocketknife, *The Elements of Style,* like most lasting literary or artistic works, also turns out to have something else going on. The whole is greater than the sum of its elements. What's behind this short book's long success?

First, *The Elements of Style* works as advertised; it's a straightforward, functional guide to clear expression. Generations of teachers credit the book for its help in the effort to unclutter and sharpen their students' prose. In my own career, editing books by subject-matter experts who sometimes have little writing experience, I have seen that recommending Strunk and White usually helps. Writers who take the book's advice to heart find that it helps them clarify their thoughts, discover the simpler line through their material, and get the right words down on paper in good order.

Second, there is an appealing complexity to the book's voice. *The Elements of Style* is sometimes mischaracterized as little more than a short list of do's and don'ts delivered in a schoolmarmish tone by two old jaspers who were simply way too sure of themselves. But a closer look reveals a greater degree of nuance, humor, and heart than that caricature admits. The book's textured voice is thanks to the characters of its coauthors. *The Elements of Style* is the product of not one mind but two, and those two further apart in temperament and effect than is usually assumed. The book doesn't speak with one monolithic, "strunkenwhite" voice. It is as multifaceted as any other product of creative collaboration. There is a head-heart, Spock-Kirk dynamic to the Strunk-White partnership, a stirring mix of reason and feeling that gives the book a very human character and creates just enough tension to keep things interesting. The charge created by these two distinct voices sparking off each other as they approach writing's basic questions is one of the book's hidden strengths and an important source of its staying power. E. B. White described Strunk's voice on the page as being "in the form of sharp commands, Sergeant Strunk snapping orders to his platoon," and it's true, the professor seems to spend much of his time in an imperative mood: "Do not break sentences in two," "Use the active voice," "Omit needless words." It's a natural enough idiom, considering his day job; Strunk sounds teacherly, though he's not without humor.

White's voice, on the other hand, is that of the writer, the practitioner of long experience whose sympathies favor the artistic side of the enterprise. In the foreword to the 1959 edition, White, in describing his Chapter V essay, "An Approach to Style," lets readers know that Strunk "had no part in this escapade, and I have no way of knowing whether he would approve." The caveat is offered because, in Chapter V, White intends to take the discussion in a new direction, and he does. In the opening paragraphs of the chapter, he is careful to explain that, while his ideas are presented as rules ("since the book is a rulebook"), he invites readers to think of them instead as "mere gentle reminders." Strunk and White's tag-team approach makes the creative whole possible. If Strunk is the master boatbuilder, teaching readers about the basic tools and techniques of the trade, White is the pilot, sharing what he has learned about getting safely out of harbor and taking the craft where he wants to go.

Finally, true believers have always felt something more, an extra dimension that has likely been a fundamental source of the book's success all along: As practical as it is for helping writers over common hurdles, *The Elements of Style* also embodies a worldview, a philosophy that, for some, is as appealing as anything either author ever managed to get down on paper. *Elements* is a credo. And it is a book of promises—the promise that creative freedom is enabled, not hindered, by putting your faith in a few helpful rules; the promise that careful, clear thinking and writing can occasionally touch truth; the promise of depth in simplicity and beauty in plainness; and the promise that by turning away from artifice and ornamentation you will find your true voice.

That's a lot of promise for such a little book. And not everyone believes it. Despite, or perhaps because of, the success it has enjoyed, *Elements* has drawn its share of critical fire over the years. Earlier, I mentioned the book's propensity for making some people nuts. Here we are. While admirers appreciate *Elements'* devotion to form and its occasionally bracing Dutch-uncle tone, those same qualities fuel most of the criticism leveled by detractors. Some writers and readers, reflexively distrustful of certainty from any quarter, reject *The Elements of Style* for the stubborn, doctrinal, vaguely medicinal air that they claim clings to it. For all its popularity, its plain common sense, and its decades of success in the classroom, it is surprising the extent to which Strunk and White have gotten up the noses of some academics and critics. In books such as *Adios, Strunk and White; Clear and Simple as the Truth;* and *The Sound on the Page,* and in the academic press, in articles with titles like "Interrogating the Popularity of Strunk and White," "A Multi-Million Dollar Hoax?" and "Ideology, Power, and Linguistic Theory," critics have attempted to knock the conceptual pins out from under this perennial best-seller. It's a critical reaction that was not unanticipated in 1959, and the fact that *The Elements of Style* succeeded not in spite of but largely *because* of its willingness to buck liberalizing trends in the humanities has, for some, been a source of considerable irritation.

The Elements of Style does, of course, have its limitations. It is neither a complete rhetoric nor an exhaustive, methodical grammar. It is a collection—some have called it a hodgepodge—of several distinct kinds of advice for writers, reflected in the titles of its five sections: "Elementary Rules of Usage" (commas, colons, subject-verb agreement, and a few other common trouble spots); "Elementary Principles of Composition" (writing's larger elements—sentences, paragraphs); "A Few Matters of Form" (the mechanics of margins, spacing, hyphens, spelling out titles and numerals, et cetera); "Words and Expressions Commonly Misused" (*effect/affect*, *lay/lie*, and the like); and "An Approach to Style" (White's twenty-page essay on fundamental aspects and attitudes of writing). Its authors would have been the first to admit that *Elements* is incomplete, idiosyncratic, opinionated, and not infallible. As strong as the book is on the whole, weaknesses can be found in each of its five sections. And some parts are more timeless than others. "Words and Expressions Commonly Misused," for instance, has been revised more thoroughly than any other section, for the simple reason that vocabulary changes relatively quickly. And for all its broad applicability, *The Elements of Style* is a resolutely personal book. On seeing it in 1957, for the first time in thirty-eight years, White was charmed, but he also noted, "Sometimes the book, like the man, seems needlessly compressed, and it is undeniably notional." The 1918 *Elements of Style* was a clear reflection of William Strunk's standards and personality, but White felt it was largely accurate in its details and astute in its attitude. He knew Strunk was on the right path. Jack Case and Macmillan, in turn, put their trust in White, and, with the addition of White's voice, the book's character came alive. If *The Elements of Style* is not unassailable in every one of its details, it pulls together as a whole, and then some, on the strength of that character.

I began the legwork for this book in the Cornell University Library's Division of Rare and Manuscript Collections, which houses E. B. White's collected letters and manuscripts. My days were spent working with the collection in the division's reading room, two levels below ground. At the time of my visit, the university was enjoying the first warm, bright days of spring. Each day at noon, I came up and out of the archive to sit in the sun on a bench near the Arts Quad and eat my lunch. Each day, the quad's lawn was filled with students. With the sudden change in weather, they had all gone over to T-shirts, shorts, and flip-flops. Bookbags and backpacks had been thrown aside, Frisbees and footballs were in the air. Dogs jumped. Music played. Groups of young men and women lounged in the grass, laughing, talking, shouting, flirting. It looked like a May Day fling in the Sheep Meadow. And it was a welcome sight, after a too-long winter. But I didn't linger outside. I stayed just long enough to finish a sandwich, eat an apple, and down a bottle of water before getting back to the archive.

Here's why: the letters. Anyone who has read the published collection, *Letters of E. B. White*, knows their addictive power. White was a master of the form, and his letters make ridiculously pleasurable reading: They're playful, sharp, and lit by White's childlike curiosity and his pragmatic but beautifully slanted sensibility. They span White's life—his family, *The New Yorker*, his books, his fans, his friends—and they run from the serious to the seriously silly. The archive is also a pointed reminder of just what we lost when we gave up writing letters. What were we thinking? I suppose we really weren't; it wasn't a conscious choice. Technology took over, and we simply outpaced the medium. Our days no longer have the kind of elbow room that letter writing requires.

I am privileged to reprint in this book letters not only from E. B. White (many never published before) but also from William Strunk Jr. and White's editors at Macmillan. White leads the pack, but all had a strong grip on the form. Strunk's letters are the correspondence of friendship: reminiscences of school days, chatting about mutual friends, books, writers, writing, and the small events of the day. The exchanges between White and Jack Case offer a look over the shoulders of author and editor at work, and details about how *The Elements of Style* was born and took shape. Today's office workers, accustomed to the staccato, dispassionate vernacular of e-mail, may marvel at the expansiveness, humor, and warmth of the White-Case letters. They are a wistful reminder of the days when business took the time to breathe.

Also in the E. B. White archive are many notes written in response to letters he received from readers of *The Elements of Style.* Shortly after the book's publication, White discovered that he had strolled onto a minefield. Letters from readers started coming in early 1959, and they were still arriving at the time of his death, twenty-six years later. Every conceivable human reaction to writing advice is represented in the letters. Some readers wrote to complain, in achingly correct prose; some sent verbal bouquets of thanks; some sent suggestions for revisions; some sent poems, essays, even homemade crossword puzzles, on the subject of style; some wanted to argue—about *got* and *gotten,* *that* and *which, he* and *she,* and just about anything else; some praised White for catching their own favorite peeves, others decried him for missing theirs; some wrote to suggest changes in English grammar or spelling, as if White were the keeper of the keys; some had been driven to insight by the text and were thankful for it; some reveled in having caught either White or Strunk violating one of his own rules. Many of the readers' more sensible suggestions and fixes were incorporated into later editions.

The letters, and the necessity of keeping up with revisions and updates for the book, sometimes tried White's patience. As early as the fall of 1959, he complained to a friend, "Life as a textbook editor is not the rosy dream you laymen think it is. I get the gaa damndest letters every day from outraged precisionists and comma snatchers, complaining every inch of the way." During his work on the second edition, he griped to another friend:

"I hate the guts of English grammar." Much, not all, of White's grumbling was tongue in cheek. It's clear he enjoyed corresponding with readers, and his replies were invariably patient, good-humored, and never less than kind. A sampling of White's notes to readers of *The Elements of Style* are sprinkled throughout the pages that follow.

When I began working on this book, one thing I knew for sure was that I wanted to include the thoughts of other writers on the subject of *The Elements of Style* and on the ideas about *Elements* that I was hoping to explore. Keeping in mind White's maxim, expressed near the end of *The Elements of Style,* that "the whole duty of a writer is to please and satisfy himself," I began with the admittedly selfish move of approaching some of my favorite writers. I was more than pleasantly surprised when most of them happily accepted the invitation. It seems that Strunk and White mean something to just about everyone who takes writing seriously, though opinions about the book are as varied as the writers themselves. A writer's presence here should not necessarily be interpreted as a full embrace of my own wild-eyed, crusading *Element*ism; the writers speak for themselves, and their voices will be heard throughout the book.

This book about *The Elements of Style* is the story of the writers and editors who created it and the influences that shaped it—of Strunk's own education and his stylistic models; of White's devotion, like that of his hero Thoreau, to the ideals of simplicity and clarity, in life and on the page; and of the blood bonds linking White's style, *The New Yorker,* and *The Elements of Style.* It is also an appreciation of the broader worldview underlying the *Elements* ethos, which includes such old-fashioned, unironic virtues as correctness, simplicity, truth, and the value of the individual voice. With my own biases laid bare, and with Mr. Strunk and Mr. White fending for themselves quite capably, it also seemed fair to let some of the academic naysayers have their (nay)say. They have strong feelings and interesting ideas about what this little book is up to.

Elements is a Rorschach of a book, and fans and critics both delight in telling what they see in it. It's only fitting that Strunk and White affect readers so variously, because their book *is* something of a hodgepodge. But in my view, and in the views of many others, it's a hodgepodge that hits the fundamentals in a memorable way, boosts the reader's faith in the aforementioned virtues, and puts writers on a path to clearer, better prose. It is not the only path available, but it is one that thousands of writers, and millions of readers, have found congenial. The *New Yorker* writer Adam Gopnik, interviewed in these pages, memorably describes *The Elements of Style* as "a very good guide to writing the kind of prose that it's a very good guide to writing." I can live with that. And for my money, *Elements* is also a very good guide to writing the kind of prose I like to read: prose that is supple enough to convey complex ideas clearly; that shuns gratuitous decoration while welcoming insight and wit; that's as lean, sturdy, and fit for its purpose as a pump handle.

I

English 8

Omit needless words.
—WILLIAM STRUNK JR.

The cost of raising William Strunk Jr. from birth to age twenty-one, including four years' tuition at the University of Cincinnati, totaled $2,140.78. This is not an approximation. The sum is entered beneath two columns of neatly penned figures—a year-by-year reckoning, to the penny, of Will Jr.–related expenses—in an account book kept by his father. An energetic record keeper all his adult life, William Strunk Sr., in a flowing, nearly calligraphic script, filled ledger after ledger with the details of Strunk family life—expenditures of every kind, from the cost of his own wedding to the annual expenses of child rearing; academic achievements of his four children (including not only degrees, awards, and honors but individual course names and grades earned, from high school through college); even vacation notes (down to shuffleboard scores on shipboard). In a lengthy ledger entry from 1920, near the end of his life, William Sr. listed and described various possessions, bits of significant family memorabilia, that he had decided to pass on to Will Jr., including a copy of *The Life of Napoleon*, a copy of *Masterpieces of European Art* ("very heavy and large volume"), one hundred dollars in Confederate notes, a two-volume history of Cincinnati, and a note from young Will's grade-school principal stating that "Willie was best in his class & best in school & [he] expected a great future for him." William Sr.'s most significant gift to his son did not make the list, though it was the bequest most surely responsible for Will Jr.'s eventual success and his posthumous fame: the Strunkian love of order, an unshakable faith in the value of getting the facts down clearly and keeping things straight.

In 1891, at twenty-two, William Strunk Jr. arrived at Cornell with a bachelor of arts degree from the University of Cincinnati and one year of teaching experience as an instructor in mathematics at Rose Polytechnic Institute in Terre Haute, Indiana. In a photograph from that year, he looks like a high schooler cleaned up for a job interview, his hair center-parted and combed flat, his gaze bright, the suggestion of a smile looming beneath an iffy mustache. On Strunk's arrival, Cornell University, the youngest of the Ivy League colleges, was only a year older than Strunk himself. Endowed by New York Senator Ezra Cornell and built on his donated farmland, the university is perched high above the city of Ithaca (Cornell students past and present speak of life "on the hill") at the southern end of Cayuga Lake, the longest of New York's Finger Lakes, which reaches forty miles north to its outflow at the Seneca River. Ezra Cornell envisioned a broad mission for the school, and his declaration from 1865 still stands as Cornell's motto: "I would found an institution where any person can find instruction in any study."

At Cornell, Strunk took up an instructorship in English and began his graduate studies. His interest in languages and

William Strunk Jr. in
1891, his first year at
Cornell
Used by permission of
Susan Beach.

literature led him to philology, a broad field that included the
close study of the history and development of language and literature, and was a precursor to modern linguistics, among other
disciplines. Strunk's graduate work at Cornell included classes
in comparative philology and grammar, Anglo-Saxon, Sanskrit,
Icelandic, and Old Bulgarian.

Will Jr.'s interest in languages had been encouraged from
an early age at home in Cincinnati. His mother, Ella Garretson Strunk, was a former teacher. His father, William Sr.—a
teacher, principal, lawyer, Civil War veteran, and son of German
immigrants—was fluently bilingual and passionate about public
education. He served on the Cincinnati board of education for
four years, on the board of examiners of public-school teachers for six years, and on the board of directors of the University
of Cincinnati for six years. William Sr. insisted on teaching his

Ella Garretson Strunk, William Strunk Sr., and William Jr.
Used by permission of Susan Beach.

children German himself, even though Cincinnati schools at that time offered bilingual instruction in German and English.

Born July 1, 1869, the eldest of four surviving children, Will Jr. was raised on Cincinnati's near northeast side, in a rambling two-and-a-half-story Queen Anne in the Walnut Hills neighborhood. His parents were both strong personalities, cultured, caring, and devoted to their children. Ella had lost several children as infants and was a protective mother; she homeschooled Will Jr. and his siblings—Howard, Ella, and Allen—at least some of the time. The family was close, but relations were formal by today's standards—William Sr. and Ella called each other "Father" and "Mother," and the children followed their example. William Sr.'s devotion to his responsibilities was also expressed in the mode of the day and as befitted his own upbringing as the son of an immigrant: with a firm hand on the family tiller and a single-minded focus on the solidity and security of his children's futures. His life followed a trajectory that was energetic and ambitious, and largely seems to have hit its mark.

A quotation that William Sr. chose to copy carefully into his ledger indicates something of the backbone-stimulating character of Will Jr.'s upbringing. The passage is by Frederic William Farrar, Archdeacon of Westminster, Dean of Canterbury, and a popular nineteenth-century writer on theology.

> Nothing is more deplorable than the feebleness, the placidity, the limpness of purpose, of many of our youths; they live from hand to mouth, without reverence, without purpose, without self-denial, without force. They are all straw, they have no iron in them. They would like distinction very well, if it dropped into their mouths; but they lack the manly fiber, the stern self-control, the never-wearied patience, the inflexible determination, the unwavering adaptation of means to ends, by which success is won.

Five years after his arrival at Cornell, Strunk received his Ph.D. His parents made the trip from Cincinnati for the occasion, and William Sr. was able to inscribe, on his ledger page detailing Will Jr.'s postgraduate career, "Doctor of Philosophy, June 18-1896." The accomplishment is set off and centered at the bottom of the page, written in a large, careful hand, and underscored by two strong red lines as straight as pinstripes.

After receiving his doctorate, Strunk resigned the instructorship in English to accept a traveling fellowship in English philology, and he spent the academic year 1898–99 at the Sorbonne and the Collège de France, Paris, where he studied the history of French verbs and of French literature, the morphology of low

Latin, medieval French literature, phonetics, and still more comparative philology. Shortly after his return from Paris, Strunk married Emilie Locke, whom he had met and fallen in love with at Cornell. A New Orleans native of English and mixed French–New England parentage, Emilie had been raised in Paris, was fluent in French and English, and had come to Ithaca around 1892 to live with her older sister, Kate, and Kate's husband, a professor of German literature. Will and Emilie were married in 1900, and their marriage was said to be a happy one. They enjoyed traveling together, and they enjoyed their three children, William Oliver, Catherine, and Edwin, each of whom pursued the Strunk legacy of academic and professional achievement into the next generation. Oliver, the eldest, became a renowned musicologist, taught at Princeton for thirty years, and wrote seminal works in his field. His *Essays on Music in the Western World* was nominated for a National Book Award, and his collection *Source Readings in Music History* is in print today, regularly revised, and still considered essential reading for students of music history. Catherine graduated from the Cornell medical school and went on to a successful career as a research pediatrician and author at Yale. Catherine's twin, Edwin, also graduated from Cornell and spent his working years as an engineer in the automotive industry. Will and Emilie did well enough on Will's salary to hire servants to help with the children and housework. Emilie did not work outside the home, but she was an active volunteer, at one time teaching sewing skills to immigrant women.

Will Strunk Jr. was liked by his students, who appreciated his sense of humor and his friendliness. He enjoyed athletics, though he was slight of build and of average height and, as an undergraduate, had occasionally written about sports for the school paper. He was known to be a fastidious dresser (few pictures seem to exist of William Strunk sans suit and tie). He didn't give

William Strunk Jr., second from left, 1896, the year he received his Ph.D.
Courtesy of the Division of Rare and Manuscript Collections, Cornell University Library.

up on the mustache, which eventually matured into a respectably thick but close-trimmed salt-and-pepper embellishment of an otherwise unadorned persona.

A reader wrote to tell White that this sentence, written by Strunk, violated its own rule: "The subject of a sentence and the principal verb should not, as a rule, be separated by a phrase or clause that can be transferred to the beginning."

Dear Mr. _____

Thanks for your letter about the sentence in Strunk. The letter comes at an opportune moment, as I am about to revise the little book for Macmillan and shall take a good look at your catch. The qualifying phrase "as a rule" saves

*the sentence from being an out-and-out violation of its own
commandment—in other words, sometimes the separation of
subject and verb is admissable, or even preferable.*

*I haven't made up my own mind yet which I like in this
case. It's even conceivable that Strunk was enjoying a little
joke when he wrote that sentence—I wouldn't put it past him.*

Sincerely,
E. B. White

A small box in the Cornell archives holds a few of Strunk's surviving papers and notebooks. They provide clear evidence of an ordered, scholarly mind singularly focused on the academic passions that drove him. His doctoral thesis is here: 155 typed, double-spaced pages titled *The Anglo-Saxon Remains of Apocryphal Acts of the Apostles,* a readable study limning the influence of the likes of Pseudo-Matthew and the Apocalypse of Paul on the likes of Bede and Cynewulf. The notebooks contain his thoughts jotted in a hasty but legible hand—small, imperfect, angular, flecked with bits of Greek, Latin, Old English—for lectures or for writing projects, notes on Kipling, Dante, Greek drama, Buddhism, Shakespeare. (Kipling was a favorite of Strunk's; he considered him a model prose writer, a master of concrete language. Snatches of Kipling were sure to appear on the sheets of admirable writing examples that he frequently handed out in class.) There is a book in the box, Walter Bronson's 1905 anthology *English Essays,* filled with Strunk's handwritten marginal notes about form, rhetoric, argument, structure, and logic in the essays of Milton, Lamb, Hazlitt, Johnson, Macaulay. Around the edges of Milton's *Areopagitica,* Strunk organized his lightly penciled notes in outline fashion:

I.   The destruction of books [is] the destruction of reason itself.
II. Censorship would deprive us of the discipline of choosing between right and wrong.
III. Censorship would lead to stagnation in religion.
IV. Censorship hinders the search for truth.

Languages, literature, drama, and writing would be Strunk's focus through the rest of his academic life. Over his nearly fifty years at Cornell, he taught a variety of courses in composition, drama, poetry, Old English, Shakespeare, Chaucer, and English usage and style. Among other extracurricular duties, Strunk served on the committee on undergraduate scholarships and the library council. He was also active in a group known as the Manuscript Club, an informal Saturday-night gathering of students and professors interested in writing. Students brought works in progress to the meetings, where they were read aloud and critiqued. The club met at the home of its founder, the English professor Martin Sampson, its stated goal, in Sampson's words: "To be frank, to use one's brains, to write what is in one to write, and never to take oneself too damned seriously or too damned lightly—these are the only articles of our creed." It was during those Saturday meetings, discussing poetry, prose, and the writer's art over light snacks and "shandygaff"—diluted beer—that Strunk developed a friendship with one of the club's most committed and talented writers, a sensitive and deeply thoughtful young man named Elwyn Brooks White.

E. B. White was born in Mount Vernon, New York, July 11, 1899, the sixth child of Samuel and Jessie White. White was, as his biographer Scott Elledge notes, "the last child of parents who loved children." His New England upbringing, at the hands of generous, forbearing, open-minded parents, encouraged his many loves—of nature, animals, travel, music, the arts, and family.

The White family, 1899. Back: Samuel, Jessie, Elwyn, Marion. Front: Lillian, Albert, Stanley, Clara
Courtesy of the Division of Rare and Manuscript Collections, Cornell University Library. Used by permission of Allene White and the estate of E. B. White.

In a 1969 interview with *The Paris Review,* White succinctly characterized his youth—a happy childhood of some privilege, but one shaded by a multiform strain of anxiety, perhaps inherited from his father, that he would carry with him throughout his life:

As a child, I was frightened but not unhappy. My parents were loving and kind. We were a large family (six children) and were a small kingdom unto ourselves. Nobody ever came to dinner. My father was formal, conservative, successful, hardworking, and worried. My mother was loving, hardworking, and retiring. We lived in a large house in a leafy suburb, where there were backyards and stables and grape arbors. I lacked for nothing except confidence. I suffered nothing except the routine terrors

of childhood: fear of the dark, fear of the future, fear of the return to school after a summer on a lake in Maine, fear of making
an appearance on a platform, fear of the lavatory in the school
basement where the slate urinals cascaded, fear that I was un-
knowing about things I should know about.

An independent spirit and a gifted, graceful writer, White en-
tered Cornell in 1917. At Cornell, he was given the nickname
Andy, after Andrew Dickson White, Cornell's cofounder and first
president. To his friends and close acquaintances, Elwyn would,
for the rest of his life, be known as Andy. He was a curious, intellectually alive student, but his studies were of less interest to him
than the school paper, *The Cornell Daily Sun,* for which he began
working as a freshman reporter his first semester at school. Eventually he was excused from the regular theme-writing requirement in his English class, presumably because of the quantity
of writing he was doing at the *Sun.* In a playful, rhyming letter
to his mother, he expressed his relief at being liberated from the
mandatory themes: "This morning came news of my utter re-
demption from deepest gloom, for I got an exemption from any
more of those weekly abortions which the English Department
deals out in large portions—which is merely to say in a casual
way, that I won't have to write so much stuff every day." It was
one of the earliest clear signals of a character trait that was to
define White throughout his life: a broad streak of quiet, deter-
mined independence that compelled him to pursue his art on his
own terms. (And, as if to offer a hopeful sign to all future writers
made fidgety by the classroom, White earned a D in his second
semester of English.)

White worked on the *Sun* throughout his college career. He
was elected to the board of editors in spring 1919, his sophomore
year, and in his junior year, he was made editor in chief. *The*

Cornell Daily Sun was no lightweight, frat-gossip student rag. As Elledge notes, it was "one of the best college papers published in America. . . . It subscribed to the AP wire service, and carried international and national news on its front page." The *Sun* also served as Ithaca's only morning newspaper. White's responsibility as editor was substantial, and he approached it as a serious means of honing his writing craft and learning the business of journalism. Decades later, following the publication of his laudatory essay about William Strunk Jr. in *The New Yorker,* White responded to a letter he had received from Strunk's younger brother Allen:

> *I managed to go through four years at Cornell without getting much of an education (I was busy with the* Sun *and couldn't be bothered), but several things happened to me in Ithaca that stood me in good stead. English 8 with Strunk is high on the list. The ideal of precision, of brevity, of clarity—it can hardly be called an education but it has been such a help. When [your brother] wasn't mesmerizing me he was making me chuckle, and the result was that he was able to implant a few indispensable truths.*

English 8—the eighth English course listed in the Cornell catalog—was officially titled English Usage and Style. It was not an entry-level class but a two-semester course in advanced writing and prose analysis that White took during his junior year. In *The Register of Cornell University* for that academic year, 1919–20, is this description:

> **8. English Usage and Style.** Throughout the year, credit three hours a term. Prerequisite, course 20, or its equivalent. The instructor's permission must be obtained before enrollment in the course. Professor STRUNK.

The prerequisite, English 20, was Nineteenth Century Prose, which itself required students to have first completed an introductory English course open "only to underclassmen who have satisfied the entrance requirement in English."

It was in English 8 that E. B. White first encountered *The Elements of Style*. Strunk had published the forty-three-page booklet himself in 1918, and it was available for purchase in the Cornell bookstore, at twenty-five cents a copy. Strunk had at least two goals in mind with the publication of *The Elements of Style*: to offer students a clear, concise blueprint revealing the main supports of what he called "plain" English style ("a few essentials," in his words) and to save himself, and other instructors, time in grading papers. Strunk's opening to the book's original first chapter ("Introductory") lays out the scope of the work:

> This book is intended for use in English courses in which the practice of composition is combined with the study of literature. It aims to give in brief space the principal requirements of plain English style. It aims to lighten the task of instructor and student by concentrating attention (in Chapters II and III) on a few essentials, the rules of usage and principles of composition most commonly violated. The numbers of the sections may be used as references in correcting manuscript.
>
> The book covers only a small portion of the field of English style, but the experience of its writer has been that once past the essentials, students profit most by individual instruction based on the problems of their own work, and that each instructor has his own body of theory, which he prefers to that offered by any textbook.

The Elements of Style was not, has never been, a guide to the details of English grammar. Readers did not learn from Strunk (or, later, from White) the difference between a noun and an adverb or how to tell a conjunction from a preposition. *Elements* assumes of its readers, as Strunk no doubt assumed of his English 8 students, a functional understanding of the language's raw materials, so that, for example, in his explanation of Rule 5, "Do not join independent clauses by a comma," he was able to proceed in confidence without stopping to define *independent clause* or, for that matter, *conjunction, compound sentence,* or *adverb.* Style, as understood by Strunk, is a matter several significant steps beyond rote knowledge of the parts of speech and basic grammatical terms.

In its 1918 incarnation, the book included six chapters:

I.   Introductory
II. Elementary Rules of Usage
III. Elementary Principles of Composition
IV. A Few Matters of Form
V.   Words and Expressions Commonly Misused
VI. Words Commonly Misspelled

Chapters II and III are where most of the action that matters—to writing, to reading—takes place. Chapter IV, "A Few Matters of Form," is just over two pages of guidance on using headings, numerals, parentheses, and quotations in text, and two pointers on the proper styling of references and titles in academic works. Chapter V offers concise usage tips for forty-nine "Words and Expressions Commonly Misused," from *all right* to *would.* Chapter VI, "Words Commonly Misspelled" is a one-pager, fifty-six words (one of them a name: Philip) in three columns. The list contains words that you wouldn't necessarily have expected early twentieth-century undergrads to have trouble with—*describe, develop, similar, tragedy, until*—but that must have turned up misspelled often enough to get under Strunk's skin.

The range of Chapter II, "Elementary Rules of Usage," is narrow; of its eight rules, five are concerned, from one angle or another, with the use of the comma, that bantam punctuation mark that fights far above its weight class, doing so much to parse and pattern expression, to delineate sense from nonsense.

The ten rules in Chapter III, "Elementary Principles of Composition," have a broader aim: the marshaling of the writer's thoughts and their successful transfer to paper with minimal loss of meaning and force. If, as William Zinsser has said, "writing is thinking on paper," Strunk's Chapter III is as much about clear thinking as it is about clear writing. It reminds writers that the effort behind good writing is the necessary and often difficult work of making choices about which ideas to retain and which to reject, about their arrangement and emphasis. The chapter is a primer on the economics of communication. *Use the active voice. Put statements in positive form. Keep related words together. Place the emphatic words of a sentence at the end.* They're habits of thought and characteristics of personality as much as they are tip's for writing a better paper. "Make definite assertions," Strunk says, and thereby suggests to readers an approach not only to cleaner, more forceful writing but to a life lived with greater confidence and intentionality. Chapter III also contains the rule and the paragraph that constitute Strunk's Sermon on the Mount, the nugget that cradles the book's DNA and that might be sufficient to reconstitute *The Elements of Style* in its entirety should the rest of it, like heaven and earth, pass away:

13. Omit needless words.

Vigorous writing is concise. A sentence should contain no unnecessary words, a paragraph no unnecessary sentences, for the same reason that a drawing should have no unnecessary lines and a machine no unnecessary parts. This requires not that the writer make all his sentences short, or that he avoid all detail and treat his subjects only in outline, but that every word tell.

ROY BLOUNT JR.

"Omit needless words." One of the great three-word sentences. Tighten it a notch or two? "Cut extra words"? No, brevity isn't everything, there's also tone.

"Omit needless words" is something I have clutched to my bosom since my tenth-grade English teacher turned me on to Strunk and White. Elegant solutions are clean, not ostentatious. Comedy especially needs to be tight. In the sense that music is tight. And I don't know that any other book could have fixed that principle in my head as firmly as *The Elements of Style.* However, comedy requires whoop-de-do as well. If the writer's juices don't get flowing, what's the point? If Fred and Ginger weren't precise, they wouldn't be dancing, but they wouldn't be glorious if they weren't lit from within. (And if Ginger weren't so damn hot.)

Needless is the right word. *Unnecessary* is three syllables longer and sounds prissy. The *need* in *needless* implies drive, impulse. If *Elements of Style* lacked that propulsion, it wouldn't still be holding people's attention.

Roy Blount Jr. is a humorist, actor, editor, reporter, and author. His latest book is *Alphabet Juice.*

Strunk did not claim to have broken new ground with *The Elements of Style.* Just the opposite. His idea was to shine a light on the scaffolding that had supported clear communication since at least the time of Aristotle, who, as early as the fourth century B.C., was reminding his readers that, among its other qualities, effective rhetoric depends on clarity, plainness of expression (preferring the ordinary word to the unusual), and naturalness. "A writer must disguise his art and give the impression of speaking naturally and not artificially," Aristotle advises in *The Art of Rhetoric.* "Naturalness is persuasive, artificiality is the contrary; for our hearers are prejudiced and think we have some design against them, as if we were mixing their wines for them." Strunk's contribution was in the choices he made about which specific "essentials" to discuss and in his own pithy modeling of the doctrines he preached. The book was also a compendium of many of the influences that had shaped Strunk's personal and professional life: For the examples in *Elements,* he drew from literature (Dickens, Hazlitt, Stevenson, Coleridge, Wordsworth, Keats, Shelley, Burns, Thackeray, and especially Shakespeare— characters from *Macbeth, Romeo and Juliet, Hamlet, Othello, Julius Caesar,* and *The Taming of the Shrew* make appearances); from American and European history (the Constitution, Columbus, Admiral Nelson, Napoleon, William Henry Harrison, Benjamin Harrison, the Sherman Act, the Duke of York, Oliver Cromwell, Churchill); and from other Western civ pillars, including Aristotle, the Bible, the *Iliad,* and the *Odyssey.* Strunk's hometown, Cincinnati, shows up, as does a ship's journey from Liverpool to New York, a voyage he had made more than once, first as a child traveling with his parents.

The Elements of Style was written at a time when learning rhetorical principles and developing a sensitivity to standard usage were assumed to be components of a liberal education. Far from foisting his own arbitrary and idiosyncratic preferences on his captive audience, Strunk was passing along standards of the culture in a way that students accepted and parents expected, and *Elements* took its place among many contemporary works with similar aims. In his introduction, he recommends a number of these other books and authors "for reference or further study." These sources offer a revealing look at the principles of usage, writing, and rhetoric that Strunk believed in.

One of the books Strunk recommends is James P. Kelley's *Workmanship in Words*, published in 1916. "If we live in the world," says Kelley, "we must use words; if we choose, we may use them well. . . . He that does anything for the right use of words does so much, directly or indirectly, for character, for conduct, for happiness." In the introduction to his book *English Usage* (1917), another of Strunk's recommendations, John Lesslie Hall seeks the source of our standards of usage and develops a view that Strunk patently shared. Usage standards aren't handed down by God, nor are they slavishly derived from logic or reason ("He who would fight custom with grammar is a fool," Montaigne said); they in fact arise more or less organically and can be derived only by seeking them out in the works of our best writers. Hall cites Quintilian, the Roman rhetorician and author of *Institutes of Oratory*: "In advising those who cultivate eloquence as to what kind of words to use," Hall writes, "[Quintilian] says that the words which they use should have *consensum eruditorum*, the consensus, agreement, of the cultivated." Hall asks his readers to agree that

> no better standard can be found than "the easy language of cultivated men who are neither specialists nor pedants." This sentence is pregnant with meaning. A specialist is apt to have "fad" words that he likes to air on occasion. A pedant is absolutely unreliable in matters of usage: he often "murders the King's English" in trying to save it. A cultivated, refined man of liberal culture not addicted to any specialty and not given to pedantry is apt to use easy and elegant language free from affectation and from priggishness.

A third recommendation from the original introduction to *The Elements of Style,* and one that appears to have had a considerable influence on Strunk, is *On the Art of Writing,* published in 1916 by Sir Arthur Quiller-Couch, a popular novelist, essayist, lecturer, and editor, born in Cornwall, who wrote under the pseudonym Q. Strunk particularly recommends a chapter from *On the Art of Writing* titled "Interlude on Jargon," and it's not hard to see the appeal the chapter held for him. In this lecture, originally delivered at Cambridge in 1913, Quiller-Couch lays out his brief against "jargon," his label for unclear, weak, or misleading writing: "It looks precise, but it is not. It is, in these times, *safe*: a thousand men have said it before and not one to your knowledge had been prosecuted for it." He points to government as a fertile field for studying jargon in all its flowering variety:

> Has a Minister to say "No" in the House of Commons? Some men are constitutionally incapable of saying no: but the Minister conveys it thus—"The answer to the question is in the negative." That means "no." Can you discover it to mean anything less, or anything more except that the speaker is a pompous person?— which was no part of the information demanded.

> That is Jargon, and it happens to be accurate. But as a rule, Jargon is by no means accurate, its method being to walk circumspectly around its target; and its faith, that having done so it has either hit the bull's eye or at least achieved something equivalent, and safer.

It's easy to imagine Strunk nodding in agreement, and to hear in Quiller-Couch the mix of conviction and authority, spiked with dry humor, that Strunk surely enjoyed and endorsed. Jargon, according to Quiller-Couch, prefers circumlocution to straight speech and "habitually chooses vague and woolly abstract nouns rather than concrete ones." The abstract noun is "a vile thing," he says. "It wraps a man's thoughts round like cotton wool." Quiller-Couch assumes "manly" writing to be the goal, and he tells readers how to achieve it:

> I shall have something to say by-and-by about the concrete noun, and how you should ever be struggling for it whether in prose or in verse. For the moment I content myself with advising you, if you would write masculine English, never to forget the old tag of your Latin Grammar—
>
> *Masculine will only be*
> *Things that you can touch and see.*
>
> . . . The first virtue, the touchstone of masculine style, is its use of the active verb and the concrete noun. When you write in the active voice, "They gave him a silver teapot," you write as a man. When you write "He was made the recipient of a silver teapot," you write jargon. But at the beginning set even higher store on the concrete noun. . . . Note how carefully the Parables—those exquisite short stories—speak only of "things which you can touch and see"—"A sower went forth to sow," "The Kingdom of Heaven is like unto leaven, which a woman took,"—and not the Parables only, but the Sermon on the Mount and almost every verse in the Gospel. . . . Or take Shakespeare. I wager you that no writer of English so constantly chooses the concrete word, in phrase after phrase forcing you to touch and see. No writer so insistently teaches the general through the particular.

It's hard now to see why writing with active verbs and concrete nouns, in a way that will make readers "touch and see," was said to be writing "as a man," but putting aside the Victorian assumption equating *good* with *manly,* it's easy enough to see that writing that's direct and specific is preferable to its opposite. And by the time these ideas are expressed through Strunk, the vestigial worry about masculinity and manliness has been dropped. This is simply how good writing works. Diffidence and timidity, on the other hand, not only result in writing that's fogged and evasive but also thin the voice, eventually effacing the writer's personality. "In literature as in life," says Quiller-Couch, in a sentiment echoed forcefully throughout Strunk, "he makes himself felt who not only calls a spade a spade but has the pluck to double spades and redouble."

IAN FRAZIER

I always thought of *The Elements of Style* as weirdly kind of related to Cornell's being an ag school. It had a plainspokenness about it that you would expect in some kind of farm manual. And that was sort of how I pictured Strunk—as a guy with straw sticking to his suit, you know? A well-dressed, kind of dusty guy who had just come in from the calving barn or something and was going to tell you something very practical. And I know that E. B. White had a kind of perverse pride in the more homespun quality of Cornell, as opposed to the fancier Ivy League schools. In my mind, *The Elements of Style* was of a piece with Robert Frost—a New England, laconic, get-to-the-point kind of book.

Ian Frazier is a longtime writer for *The New Yorker.* His most recent book is *Lamentations of the Father.*

An important, in fact axiomatic, element broached in *On the Art of Writing,* and one that floats just beneath the surface of *The Elements of Style,* is the connection between a writer's work and his moral purpose. The idea, implicit in Strunk and glimpsed plainly if only briefly in E. B. White's revision, is that writing, like most other human endeavors, is an activity with moral implications and that better writers, *good* writers, seek to shake the cant, evasiveness, and imprecision from their prose not simply because doing so makes for easier reading but because they're working in the service of truth. Strunk did not inherit this idea from his "Q" source; it was clearly a belief he held strongly, one he had likely received as a child. But Quiller-Couch, in the closing paragraph of his chapter on jargon, spells out the connection with an explicitness that Strunk chose not to:

> A lesson about writing your language may go deeper than language; for language is your reason, your *logos.* So long as you prefer abstract words, which express other men's summarised concepts of things, to concrete ones which lie as near as can be reached to things themselves and are the firsthand material for your thoughts, you will remain, at the best, writers at secondhand. If your language be jargon, your intellect, if not your whole character, will almost certainly correspond. Where your mind should go straight, it will dodge: the difficulties it should approach with a fair front and grip with a firm hand it will be seeking to evade or circumvent. For the style is the man, and where a man's treasure is there his heart, and his brain, and his writing, will be also.

E. B. White remembered English 8 less for his first encounter with *The Elements of Style* than for the teacher. In his admiring portrait of Strunk, published thirty-eight years later in *The New*

Yorker, White describes his old professor as "a memorable man, friendly and funny." He admired Strunk's self-confidence, his kindness, his sympathy for readers, his resolve, and his boldness. "Will knew where he stood," White wrote. "He was so sure of where he stood, and made his position so clear and so plausible, that his peculiar stance has continued to invigorate me—and, I am sure, thousands of other ex-students—during the years that have intervened since our first encounter."

The year White took English 8, 1919, was also the year he joined the Manuscript Club, the writers' group in which he and Strunk began the friendship that was to last until Strunk's death in 1946. White was a regular visitor at the homes of several favorite professors, including Martin Sampson and the journalism professor Bristow Adams. He was also a frequent visitor at the home of Will and Emilie Strunk, where, among other entertain-

E. B. White, Cornell
undergraduate
*Used by permission of Allene White and
the estate of E. B. White.*

ments, such as listening to music and talking about writing, he enjoyed playing chess with Strunk. Will Strunk was a strong chess player, and as a young man had once placed second in a statewide competition in Ohio. White was a good enough player to make Strunk work at it, and Strunk's son Edwin later recalled watching the two men play, his father concentrating fiercely, holding his head in both hands. White also escorted Strunk's only daughter, Catherine, on at least one date.

It would be inaccurate to suggest that White learned to write from William Strunk, though Strunk's strong opinions no doubt encouraged White's own love of the language and his ideas about the value of writing as an artistic and professional pursuit. White had been a practitioner from his youth, and the truth is, his gracefulness as a writer seemed almost to come to him by means of grace itself. A dip into the earliest pages of the *Letters of E. B. White* reveals that young Elwyn was crafting limpid, springy prose from his early teens, and he seems to have been born to it. He once wrote to his brother Stanley that "I can remember, really quite distinctly, looking a sheet of paper square in the eyes when I was seven or eight years old and thinking 'This is where I belong, this is it.'"

E. B. White went on to become one of the best-loved essayists and children's authors of the twentieth century. His publications include anthologies of his work from *The New Yorker* (such as *The Second Tree from the Corner* and *The Points of My Compass*); *One Man's Meat,* a collection of monthly columns written for *Harper's Magazine;* and the children's classics *Charlotte's Web, Stuart Little,* and *The Trumpet of the Swan.* His collected correspondence, *Letters of E. B. White,* was first published in 1976 and revised and republished in 2006 to include letters written up to his death in 1985. White received many awards for his writing, and in 1978 was given a special Pulitzer Prize for his "letters, essays and the full body of his work."

Strunk, too, was well published during his career. In addition to *The Elements of Style,* which appeared in at least three editions before his death in 1946 (the latest in 1935), he published *English Metres,* a study of the fundamentals of poetic metrical form (and, at sixty-one pages, another sharp blast of literary concision), and compiled and edited critical editions of Cynewulf's *Juliana,* John Dryden's *Essays on the Drama,* Macaulay's and Carlyle's *Essays on Samuel Johnson,* James Fenimore Cooper's *The Last of the Mohicans,* Dryden's *All for Love* and *The Spanish Fryar,* and several of Shakespeare's plays.

After White's graduation, Strunk followed White's career with enthusiasm, and they exchanged letters frequently. Strunk would bring White up to date on goings-on around the Cornell campus and offer critiques and commentary about things he'd read in *The New Yorker.* He would even occasionally send ideas for articles. In what was likely one of his last letters to White, written in November 1945, Strunk, in a deteriorating, indistinct hand, congratulated White on the publication of *Stuart Little* and told him that Professor Sampson's widow was selling her home and had handed over to Strunk all the student papers from the Manuscript Club that had piled up at the house over the years. He asked White if he wanted his old college papers back:

Of course I do not intend to preserve the collection for posterity. Most of it will go to the salvage campaign, but I was thinking of sending some back to the writers, if they would like to have them. They have all been unclaimed for a long time, so that I am discarding most of the contributions without any pangs of conscience (this doesn't include yours, of course).

2

The Steel and the Music

Strunk proved a great success as Master of Ceremonies.
He kept things moving, and enforced the rules strictly,
yet without friction in any direction.

—"Field Day Notes," *The McMicken Review,*
University of Cincinnati, June 1890

The Elements of Style is genetically linked with one of America's most well-known periodicals, *The New Yorker,* a magazine celebrated for its smart humor, its craft-conscious nonfiction and reportage, its short stories, reviews, poems, and cartoons. E. B. White did more than any other single writer to establish the tone and voice of *The New Yorker,* particularly in the magazine's critical early years. As the playwright Marc Connelly has described it, White "brought the steel and the music to the magazine." And despite the intervening decades, several changes in editorship, and the many writers who have passed through its pages, White's influence is still felt at the magazine today. *The New Yorker,* in turn, exerted its own influence on White, and his associations with the editors and other writers at the magazine were the formative relationships of his adult life, both professionally and personally. *The New Yorker* is where White tested and perfected his ideas about style, shaping the standards that he would eventually collect and summarize in *The Elements of Style*. If not for *The New Yorker;* the spirit and influence of its founding editor, Harold Ross; and White's own work at the magazine, *The Elements of Style* as unparalleled American publishing phenomenon would almost certainly never have happened.

In retrospect, E. B. White's path to *The New Yorker* seems fated. But in the five-year interval between finishing at Cornell and arriving on the doorstep of Harold Ross's fledgling magazine, White's career trajectory was a meander. After his graduation in 1921 and a summer spent working as a counselor at a camp in Ontario, he came home to live with his parents in Mount Vernon, New York, and began looking for work as a writer in Manhattan. His first job, editing copy for the United Press, lasted less than a month. He held another job, writing PR for a silk mill, for a few short weeks. For a time, he worked for the American Legion News Service, again doing mostly public relations writing. White chafed at the constraints of such work and wrote poems and short pieces on the side to please himself and for occasional publication.

Unhappy and unsettled, craving independence, and with an urge to wander and experience more of the world, White quit his job, and, in March 1922, he and a friend from Cornell, Howard Cushman, headed west on a cross-country trek in White's Model T Ford. The two worked their way across the country, with forays into Canada, selling occasional pieces to newspapers and magazines, and subsisting on infrequent gifts of cash sent from home and the sporadic, meager income from a range of odd jobs, from dishwashing to piano playing to selling roach powder. Shortly after they arrived in Seattle, in September 1922,

Cushman returned east, but White stayed on, working as a reporter for *The Seattle Times*. Both he and his editor soon agreed that White was better suited for feature writing than for hard news reporting, and he was eventually given a personal column in which he could publish poems and short essays on topics that interested him. He worked at *The Seattle Times* for nine months before being let go as part of a general layoff in June 1923. A month later, he sailed on the cruise ship SS *Buford* to Skagway, Alaska, where he talked his way into a job working in the ship's saloon and as a mess boy until the cruise returned to Seattle in September. Shortly thereafter, with no prospects and no ties keeping him in the Northwest, he returned to Mount Vernon, and to his parents' home.

In the summer of 1922, while White was still on the road with Howard Cushman, William Strunk, apparently with hopes of helping his young friend return east and settle into a career, wrote to let him know of a job lead. Strunk told White that he had talked with another Cornell graduate now working at an ad agency in New York:

July 9/22

Dear Andy,—

I had a talk recently with Mr. J. K. Fraser, C.U. '97, of the Blackman-Ross Co., advertising, 116 W. 42nd St., the upshot being that if you were inclined to go into advertising, you might present yourself to him on your return East, with the prospect that he could find a place for you, either with his own firm or with another. I assured him that you could write good English and that you had ideas, the two main points on which he wished to be assured. If, as aforesaid, you are inclined to go into advertising, I should recommend you to take Mr. Fraser up. I don't know whether or not you will think it best to send him a note in advance

or to wait until you see him. If the former, I may mention that he
will be favorably impressed by brevity.

BA assures me that you are enjoying your trip. Best regards,
and the same to Cushman. Send me a postcard from Medicine
Hat.

> *Yours as ever,*
> *W. Strunk, jr.*

Back home in New York late in 1923, after stopping in Ithaca
and visiting with friends, including Strunk, White did take a
job in advertising, with the Frank Seaman agency in Manhattan. The pay was low, White was soon bored by the work, and
he had no stomach for the adman's prime directive: selling
("I couldn't seem to make myself care whether a product got
moved or not," he later wrote). He continued writing on the
side and was occasionally published in periodicals around New
York—most regularly, and most satisfyingly, in Franklin Pierce
Adams's popular column "The Conning Tower" in the *New York
World.*

As White was struggling to find his place as a writer in New
York, Harold Ross—a former newspaperman and former managing editor of *Stars and Stripes,* the Army's newspaper for enlisted men—was laboring to develop and attract backing for a
weekly magazine combining humor with genteel big-city sophistication. In the fall of 1924, Ross circulated a prospectus about
the magazine he hoped to publish. Its first paragraph reads like
a sort of literary bat signal that must surely have twiddled the
antennae of E. B. White as he worked over his desk in the Frank
Seaman agency. Ross wrote:

The New Yorker will be a reflection in word and picture of metropolitan life. It will be human. Its general tenor will be one of gaiety, wit and satire, but it will be more than a jester. It will not be what is commonly called radical or highbrow. It will be what is commonly called sophisticated, in that it will assume a reasonable degree of enlightenment on the part of its readers. It will hate bunk.

The paragraph neatly modeled its own sentiment and reflected the taste and tone of Ross, a unique light in the history of American publishing. And all of it, from the promise of humanness to the line about bunk, described the sort of writing that E. B. White was born for.

Leavened by the financial backing of Raoul Fleischmann, nephew of the founders of America's yeast dynasty, Ross's *New Yorker* first arrived on newsstands February 17, 1925. White read the inaugural issue with interest, and his first freelance piece for the magazine, a paean to the arrival of spring written in adman's argot, appeared not long after, in the April 11 issue.

The founder of America's most urbane metropolitan weekly was neither a city boy nor particularly urbane. Born in Aspen, Colorado, in 1892, Harold Ross left school in the tenth grade to travel and work on a series of newspapers as a "tramp" journalist—a freelance, itinerant reporter—before joining the Army. He was street-smart, curious about everything, well traveled, largely self-made, and he had a strong entrepreneurial bent, but he was unpolished in ways that seemed ill-suited to his aims in the New York literary world. In his biography of the famous editor, *Genius in Disguise: Harold Ross of The New Yorker,* Thomas Kunkel writes of "Ross's gat-tooth countenance and curious behavior—long periods of quiet punctuated by 'teamsterlike snorts' or explosive, left-field interjections. He did not seem as intellectually agile as his friends." Ross was far keener than first impressions allowed, however, and he pursued his vision for *The New Yorker* with a potent mix of indefatigability and native intelligence.

Dear Prof _____

  Maybe we ought to strike a bargain: I'll remove some superfluous words if you'll remove the letter "e" from "useage." I mean the first "e"—the second one looks pretty good.

                    Yrs,
                    E. B. White

P.S. I wouldn't be bringing this up, but the word occurred three times in your letter, which means that there's a total of three "e's" that have to go.

E. B. White quit his job with Seaman's in the summer of 1925 and moved from his parents' home in Mount Vernon to share an apartment in Greenwich Village with three fraternity brothers. In October, he took a part-time job with another advertising agency, J. H. Newmark, and continued selling short pieces to *The New Yorker*. It wasn't long before Harold Ross (with the counsel of his trusted editorial assistant, Katharine Angell, *The New Yorker*'s first and most influential fiction editor and, as it happened, the future Mrs. White) recognized E. B. White as the pitch-perfect voice he had been waiting for. Ross hired White as a part-time staff writer in the fall of 1926 and brought him on full-time in early 1927.

After a shaky start, and a string of emergency cash infusions from Fleischmann and others, *The New Yorker* quickly found both its voice and its market. Circulation and ad sales climbed, hand in hand, and by 1930 White's work was reaching an audience of 100,000 readers every week in combined subscription and newsstand sales. *The New Yorker* rose to become one of the most influential and respected magazines of the twentieth century, pioneering new approaches to fiction, humor, and illustration, and publishing important nonfiction, from in-depth profiles of moguls such as William Randolph Hearst and Henry Luce to the kind of weighty reportage exemplified by John Hersey's "Hiroshima," to which an entire issue was devoted in August 1946. Throughout much of the century, *The New Yorker* was, as Ross had promised in the prospectus of 1924, "so entertaining and informative as to be a necessity for the person who knows his way about or wants to."

White married Katharine Angell in 1929 after what he later described as a "stormy" romance (when they met, she was in a failing marriage and had two children). White later wrote, "I soon realized I had made no mistake in my choice of a wife. I was helping her pack an overnight bag one afternoon when she said, 'Put in some tooth twine.' I knew then that a girl who called dental floss tooth twine was the girl for me." The Whites had one child together, Joel, born in 1930. (Until the 1999 updating of the fourth edition of *The Elements of Style*, the Whites' wedding day was memorialized as an example in Chapter I, Rule 3, "Enclose parenthetic expressions between commas": "Wednesday, November 13, 1929.") Katharine was an unusually gifted editor and a formidable intellectual force, and she is often given equal credit, with Ross, for the early survival and success of *The New Yorker*. Katharine is well known for having brought to the magazine and nurtured an astounding number of world-class writers, including James Thurber, Vladimir Nabokov, Marianne Moore, John O'Hara, Jean Stafford, William Maxwell, Ogden Nash, John Cheever, and John Updike.

E. B. White would write for *The New Yorker* for almost the rest of his life. Alec Wilkinson, a staff writer there since 1980, describes White's effect on the magazine: "Of course, White was incredibly influential in the tone *The New Yorker* took. Other people were very influential, too, but I think Harold Ross felt that something about the way White wrote—that sort of offhand, funny, unassuming, very smart writing—was exactly what he was looking for, which is probably why White found 'Notes and Comment' his home for so long. He had that straightforward prose that was exceptionally polished without appearing to be polished at all or, rather, without giving the impression of *labor;* it certainly gave the impression of being polished, but as if no effort had gone into making it that way. That was a hallmark of a certain strain of writing in *The New Yorker.* It wasn't emblematic of the entire magazine, but it was emblematic of more of the magazine than anybody else could claim to have influenced, I would think."

Wilkinson's colleague at *The New Yorker* Adam Gopnik says White's characteristic voice was an unusual combination of elements. "White's genius was for a funny kind of mixture of irony and sentiment. He's a wonderfully deflating writer. If you read through some of his collected 'Notes and Comment' pieces, which I love, they always have a lovely deflating quality, a lovely satiric quality, whether he's mocking businessmen's prose or the cult of efficiency or Khrushchev's politics. He's a satirist in that way. But he's also, in the best possible way, a sentimentalist. He always gives a tender turn to his irony at the end of everything. And I'm ravished by the resourcefulness with which he does that. He combines the satiric and the romantic in these perfect little miniatures in a way that I find immensely moving and inspiring."

As we spoke, Gopnik retrieved a favorite book, E. B. White's *Writings from The New Yorker: 1925–1976,* and read aloud an example, written in 1955:

> The two moments when New York seems most desirable, when the splendor falls all round about and the city looks like a girl

with leaves in her hair, are just as you are leaving and must say goodbye, and just as you return and can say hello. We had one such moment of infatuation not long ago on a warm, airless evening in town, before taking leave of these shores to try another city and another country for a while.... There was nothing about the occasion that distinguished it from many another city evening, nothing in particular that we can point to to corroborate our emotion. Yet we somehow tasted New York on our tongue in a great, overpowering draught, and felt that to sail away from so intoxicating a place would be unbearable, even for a brief spell.

"That kind of small-scale, petit point romantic view of the world is one I find enormously touching," Gopnik says, "particularly because it's not large-scale American romanticism. It's romanticism without bombast or loud talking. It's miniature and internal and precise."

The notion of style that White was honing with such skill and deploying in the service of *The New Yorker*—the attitudes and approaches that worked for him—would eventually be codified, to the extent that lightning can be successfully bottled, in Chapter V of *The Elements of Style*.

THOMAS KUNKEL

Harold Ross considered E. B. White a gift that fell out of the sky from heaven. Ross was basically trying to invent a new kind of writing and a new kind of tone, and in his head he knew what he wanted, but it didn't exist. Think how difficult it must have been for him to articulate that, and then to find someone who could understand what he was looking for and translate it onto the page. And suddenly there's this kid who's working at an ad agency, who starts submitting these "casuals," as they were called. They were clear, yet sophisticated. Witty without being over the top. It was a *eureka* moment for Ross and Katharine Angell, who was then helping him try to find talent. Ross realized, "Here's somebody who's putting on the page what I've been thinking in my head; I've got to get this guy."

And the converse is just as true: It's 1926, White is in his mid-twenties, he's consigned to the hell of writing advertising copy, and suddenly he's presented with the opportunity to write anything he wants, the way he wants it, about sophisticated ideas, in a magazine that in fairly short order had an important audience, and nobody screwing with him. For a writer, does it get any better than that? So from White's point of view, it must have been as though Harold Ross had fallen out of heaven for him. And once White had established that the magazine was going to survive and that it was a good fit for him, he threw in with Ross and never looked back.

Thomas Kunkel is the president of St. Norbert College in De Pere, Wisconsin. He is the author of *Genius in Disguise: Harold Ross of The New Yorker* and the editor of Ross's collected correspondence, *Letters from the Editor*. His other books include *Enormous Prayers: A Journey into the Priesthood* and, as editor, *Breach of Faith* and *Leaving Readers Behind*.

E. B. White and Harold Ross enjoyed a successful twenty-five-year working relationship, though the two were temperamentally at right angles. The high-spirited, thrice-married Ross was loquacious, was blunt to the point of boorishness, enjoyed associating with starlets and celebrity friends, from James Cagney to Harpo Marx, and was famously foulmouthed (his daughter's first word was said to be *goddammit*). White was shy and usually quiet around strangers, and he assiduously ducked the limelight everywhere but on the printed page. But both were deeply thoughtful, humorous men who shared a devotion to language, to writing, to clarity and precision of expression. White did not learn to write from Ross—White was a master craftsman his first day on the job—but it's reasonable to assume that Ross's fanaticism about language, his drive for correctness and transparency in writing, reinforced White's own convictions about good writing. And it's clear the two shared an ethos about the work they were doing together, about the care that writing and publishing required and that readers deserved, an ethos that influenced not only the course of *The New Yorker* and White's own writing but *The Elements of Style,* and, through *Elements,* millions of American readers and writers.

ADAM GOPNIK

One of the things that's always been true is that everybody at *The New Yorker* always denies that there is a *New Yorker* style. And if you look at the range of writers who have written for *The New Yorker*—from White, Thurber, Perelman, and Liebling to David Remnick to Malcolm Gladwell—there doesn't seem to be any common style there. Some of those are immensely complicated, baroque, metaphorical writers, like Liebling and Perelman. Some of them are monosyllabic, simple writers, like White and Joe Mitchell. So I don't know that there is a *New Yorker* style that could've been exuded out into a set of rules on the page. I certainly think that the rules in *The Elements of Style* are close to, are relevant to, White's own particular version of *New Yorker* style, which involved exactly those virtues of simplicity and lucidity and a kind of quiet irony illuminating everything.

[As to White's influence at the magazine today,] I think that some part of it is just common coin. In other words, for instance, a lot of the things that Ann Goldstein [head of *The New Yorker*'s copy department] tries to do to untangle writers' sentences, to press and iron writers' prose, mine included, are almost, at a folk level, just ways of Whitening, so to speak, their prose. So I think it operates at that level. But in terms of conscious emulation or imitation, I suspect there aren't very many people who are aware of it.

Adam Gopnik is an award-winning staff writer for *The New Yorker*. His most recent book is *Angels and Ages*.

A crucial aspect of Ross's genius was his ability to spot talent, coupled with the willingness to grant strong writers wide leeway in creative matters. "Ross had," White wrote years later, "a complete respect for the work and ideas and opinions of others." At the same time, both men recognized that even the most original writers, and the magazines that published them, necessarily played by a set of ground rules. Ross's preferred usage guide was the English lexicographer Henry Watson Fowler's *Dictionary of Modern English Usage* (often known simply as *Fowler*). Published in 1926, it was an encyclopedic reference that took unapologetically prescriptivist positions on many (not all) matters of usage and was enlivened by Fowler's droll, idiosyncratic style. Eleven years William Strunk's senior, H. W. Fowler was clearly an ideological brother-in-arms; in an earlier work, *The King's English*, Fowler had written:

> Any one who wishes to become a good writer should endeavor,
> before he allows himself to be tempted by the more showy quali
> ties, to be direct, simple, brief, vigorous, and lucid.

"Ross craved order," says Thomas Kunkel. "He was also largely an autodidact, and he was always defensive about his lack of formal education. I think he took *Fowler* to heart in part because it provided such a clear road map, and because he knew that if he more or less followed those rules of language he would lessen his chances of embarrassing himself for his lack of education. He loved language, and I think that, for the same reason he wanted language to be clear, he also wanted it to be appropriately punctuated, grammatically correct, and all that. *Fowler* satisfied his sense of order, and it comforted him."

In addition, the *Dictionary of Modern English Usage* provided Ross and his writers with a clearly lined playing field onto which could be deployed the great variety of things he wanted *The New Yorker* to do and be. "Ross's curiosity was so wide-ranging," says Kunkel. "He was interested in everything, and his curiosity and his sense of what he wanted the magazine to cover ran wild. I think he was comforted somewhat, again, by the fact that, no matter what was being written about, it could at least be grounded in a common set of rules, in a common usage guide, in a uniform sense of clarity that *Fowler* helped to establish."

IAN FRAZIER

For my father's generation, and for the generation that founded *The New Yorker,* which is actually the generation before my father's, the book was *Fowler,* and I could never make head or tail of *Fowler.* My dad would say, "Oh yeah, you've got to have a *Fowler.*" He gave me one and I still have it. And I've never used it for anything. *Fowler* is more about *England* English, but there was never a doubt about the Americanness of *The Elements of Style.* That was American.

Having been raised with no formal religion, Harold Ross was known to have little knowledge of the Bible, and the *Dictionary of Modern English Usage* may have been as close as he came to finding a scripture he could put his faith in. In a "Notes and Comment" essay from *The New Yorker*'s 1948 Christmas-week issue, E. B. White has fun tweaking Ross's near-religious devotion to the book, recounting an imagined office conversation in which Ross, *Fowler,* the Bible, and the Christmas story playfully intertwine. The essay opens with Ross scrooging into White's office, griping about the inanities and annoyances of the Christmas season. White is at his typewriter, a copy of *Fowler* on his desk. Ross spies the book and, softening, picks it up and begins browsing through it and quoting passages aloud.

"Greatest collection of essays and opinions ever assembled between covers," he shouted, "including a truly masterful study of *that* and *which.*"

White's half of the ensuing conversation consists of verses from Matthew's Nativity narrative offered as illustrations of the style tidbits Ross is quoting from *Fowler*. By the end of the essay, Ross's spirit has lifted, thanks less to the Good News than to Fowler's bracing good sense, and he happily pronounces the *Dictionary of Modern English Usage* "the greatest damn book ever written."

A letter written by White in 1932 mentions that Will Strunk had recently visited White in New York, so it's possible that Ross and Strunk met at least once. There is no record of what these two standard-bearers of lucidity, concision, and directness might have made of one another, though I like to imagine a conversation that was suitably clear, brief, and emphatic.

Harold Ross died at age fifty-nine in 1951, six years before White's work on the revision of *The Elements of Style* began. But it's likely that, had he lived to see it, Ross would have embraced the result of the Strunk-White collaboration as a worthy successor to the *Dictionary of Modern English Usage*, a newer testament for writers, the creed of clarity and precision pressed down, distilled to its essence, and brought up to date. He also would have recognized it as a reasonably faithful description of White's own process for forging the "steel and music" he had contributed to *The New Yorker*.

Like Harold Ross and his feelings for *Fowler*, many *Elements of Style* enthusiasts regard Strunk and White's little book as something akin to scripture, and feeling for it is sometimes expressed in quasi-religious terms. It is carried in pockets and purses, consulted when things aren't going right, reread at regular intervals, handed down from parent to child, preached with fervor by devotees, and received with gratitude by acolytes. And, as with scripture, some find its overall premise vexing. The claim that some ways of doing things, whether in writing or in getting along with thy neighbor, might actually be better than others affects some people like loose hairs under the shirt collar. But believing in Strunk and White means believing that guidelines are important—that creative freedom is enhanced, not hindered, by putting your faith in a sensible and helpful set of rules. "Strunk was a fundamentalist; he believed in right and wrong, and so, in the main, do I," wrote E. B. White. "Unless someone is willing to entertain notions of superiority, the English language disintegrates, just as a home disintegrates unless someone in the family sets standards of good taste, good conduct, and simple justice."

Of course both authors were well aware that language changes continually. *The Elements of Style* was never intended to freeze English in its tracks. The book was, after all, republished with revisions at least twice in Strunk's lifetime (by Harcourt, Brace, in 1920 and 1935), well before White became his collaborator. And following the initial revision and publication of spring 1959, E. B. White undertook full revisions of *Elements* two more times, in 1972 and 1979 (along with making numerous smaller changes to fix problems discovered between printings). If his editors at Macmillan had had their way, the revisions would have begun earlier and been issued more frequently. But the changes White made from one edition to the next were far from wholesale and, more than anything else, were focused on restating the argument and its examples in a modern idiom. The glory of Strunk's *Elements*—the whole point of reissuing it at all—was that its core advice was sound.

In his 1959 revision of Strunk's original, White clarified the text where necessary and modernized the examples; beefed up and streamlined the section on structure and organization in Chapter II, "Elementary Principles of Composition" (the 1959 revision left the Introduction unnumbered, so all chapter numbers shifted downward by one), adding Rule 8 ("Choose a suitable design and hold to it") and Rule 12 ("Use definite, specific, concrete language"); expanded Chapter III, "A Few Matters of Form"; substantially updated Chapter IV, "Words and Expressions Commonly Misused"; and added the essay that constitutes Chapter V, "An Approach to Style." The addition of White's voice and sensibility to the book simultaneously broadened and tightened the discussion, but even after a year of tinkering with the text and expanding the book by twenty-eight pages, nearly all of Strunk's original rules were left intact, in both word and spirit, including the one that continues to ring like a Lao Tzu aphorism at the book's center, the Strunkian equivalent of the Golden Rule: "Omit needless words." All of Will Strunk's fundamental principles—about precision, clarity, and brevity; about the utility of a handful of commonsense grammatical do's and don'ts; about the need for writers to be confident and forthright in their work—survived each of White's revisions, and they remain the book's sturdy scaffolding.

FRANK MCCOURT

If you're E. E. Cummings or Joyce or someone like that, you can play around because you already know the rules. You're completely disciplined in it, so you can play around. But you have to know the language first; otherwise it's just a lot of blather.

Frank McCourt's books include *Angela's Ashes*, *'Tis*, and *Teacher Man*.

Our attraction to pithy, pragmatic collections of rules seems to be written into our DNA (itself the original to-do list). Consider: the Decalogue—Moses' big ten, carved, none too subtly, in stone; the Rule of St. Benedict—the logistics of *ora et labora* for the monastic set (in a Strunkish stroke of self-effacement, Benedict referred to his manual as the "little" rule for beginners); George Washington's *Rules of Civility & Decent Behaviour in Company and Conversation* (Number 4: "In the Presence of Others Sing not to yourself with a humming Noise, nor Drum with your Fingers or Feet"); Ben Franklin's thirteen virtues ("Eat not to dullness; drink not to elevation," advised the gout-stricken gourmand); Epictetus's *Encheiridion; Robert's Rules of Order;* Buddha's Noble Eightfold Path; Paul Simon's "Fifty Ways to Leave Your Lover"; stop, drop, and roll; lather, rinse, repeat. Enumerated lists of guidelines speak to some part of our psyche that recognizes we can't get on with the complexities of anything—writing, thinking, working, playing, for some of us even shampooing—without first coming to grips with a few ground rules.

For many writers, *The Elements of Style* has the force of natural law—that law (moral and otherwise) arising from our nature as human beings. By this view, the rules codified by Strunk and polished by White are not so much *prescriptive* (i.e., telling what writing ought to be) as *descriptive* (telling how good writing does, in fact, work). A writer's freedom within these rules is like the freedom of a bird in air, which is both bounded and enabled by the laws of nature—gravity, friction, the forces of wind and air pressure—and relies on them to get where it's going. Writers can, should, and do fly off in every conceivable direction, but they do so thanks to the purchase provided by an enabling set of rules.

Professor Michael Carson of the University of Evansville, a writer, poet, and teacher of literature and writing for more than

THOMAS KUNKEL

I find it helpful sometimes to think about writing in terms of other art forms. Picasso was probably a genius from the moment he first started painting. But I'll bet that in the beginning he didn't know that blue and yellow make green, and that you use the camel hair brush for this, and the other brush for that, and all the rest. Or it's like practicing scales or études when you're learning a musical instrument. Once you've learned how to play the trumpet by practicing for five or six years, then you'll have the confidence to start messing with jazz riffs and improvising, which you can't do without a really solid foundation. You have to learn the basics. A lot of people teach themselves, but to the extent that somebody who comes before can set down these commonsense guidelines, it can save the rest of us a lot of trouble.

thirty-five years, points to the Aristotelian nature of the truths that Strunk had put his finger on: "Strunk didn't invent the rules, he just identified them—they're built into the language. If you want to build a good chair, you've got to figure out how chairs work. In the same way, you've got to figure out how language works in order to use it. So much of good writing is intangible, unknowable. But much of it *is* learnable. The guys who know the most about how to swing a bat are the ones who hit the most home runs. Someone once told Jack Nicklaus that he shot lucky. He replied, 'Yeah, and I notice that the more I practice, the luckier I get.' Strunk is just pointing out how writing works—he's descriptive, not prescriptive. And he goes right back to Aristotle. It's come down through the ages. You can't beat it."

From a letter to a reader, written by Jack Case, White's editor at Macmillan:

Why all the fuss? Because sloppy usage drives out meaning. Take a clause such as ". . . while the President hopefully approaches negotiations." Knowing that the word [hopefully] has become widely misused, one can't tell whether in this instance it applies to the President's state of mind or the writer's. One has to try to estimate whether the writer is usually careful, or usually careless, or subject to occasional wild lapses. Result: muddle, waste, frustration, murk. Ordinary good writing is supposed to transmit meaning, to enlighten and clarify, not to mumble in the dark, multiplying puzzlement. That's why.

> *Sincerely,*
> *J. G. Case*
> *Editor*

In the foreword to the current edition of *The Elements of Style*, E. B. White's stepson, the longtime *New Yorker* writer and editor Roger Angell, describes the necessity and utility of Strunk and White's "gentle reminders" with Tao-like simplicity: "They help—they really do. They work. They are the way."

RULES

I talked with writers about the most basic of Strunk and White's underlying assumptions: that creativity is empowered, rather than hampered, by working from a sensible set of rules. We talked about their own conceptions of writing's "rules" and the guidelines they keep in mind as they do their work.

Alec Wilkinson has been a staff writer for *The New Yorker* since 1980 and is the author of many books, including *Moonshine, A Violent Act, My Mentor,* and *The Protest Singer.* He has been honored with a Guggenheim Fellowship, the Robert F. Kennedy Book Award, and a Lyndhurst Prize.

"The process of creativity, in any endeavor, is a matter of making choices. Am I going to use red here—a shade of red—or will I use blue or green? Is this passage going to be in C minor or C major? You just simply have to know what you're doing. There are no examples of great work done by people who did not know what they were doing. There's nothing that can be created without a choice being made, and knowing what will allow you to deliver your intentions with the greatest impact is part of being an artist."

Wilkinson says he doesn't think about "rules" when he's writing.

"I guess I've absorbed it sufficiently that I don't much think about it. But one guideline, and this is covered in *The Elements of Style*, is the instruction to make every word count—the idea that superfluous words only undermine your intention. And if what you're trying to do is dramatize material, then you're going to undramatize it to the degree that you aren't able to do it efficiently. And by that I don't necessarily mean *succinctly*, because *efficiently* can imply that a very, very long passage of many pages needs to be handled in a certain manner. It doesn't mean that the passage of many pages should necessarily be two pages—that's different; that's a matter of pacing. Somewhere—I think in his *Paris Review* interview—William Maxwell is asked what it is that defines *New Yorker* writing, and he says that it is the intention to advance the narrative word by word as opposed to paragraph by paragraph or page by page. That's very much *New Yorker* house style, even with writers as ornate in their fashion as Nabokov or Salinger; you don't read through any of their paragraphs and think, Well, we didn't really need *this*, you know? Certain writers undermine the caution that most adjectives and adverbs are unnecessary. But it all tends to advance word by word, and that's certainly something I try to do. Probably any writer tries to do it that way if he or she is taking his or her work seriously."

Dave Barry is a Pulitzer Prize–winning humor writer whose column appeared in more than five hundred newspapers for twenty-five years. He is also the author of more than thirty books, including *Dave Barry's History of the Millennium (So Far)*, *Dave Barry on Dads*, and *Boogers Are My Beat*.

"I'm a big believer in grammar. I taught effective writing seminars when I was fairly young; I was in my twenties when I started. A lot of the people I was teaching were older than I was and had been in business a lot longer than I had, had advanced degrees, which I didn't, and really didn't know why they should listen to this kid talking to them about writing. And one of the ways I prepared for that was by learning grammar pretty thoroughly. I bought a lot of grammar texts, and I immersed myself in them. I learned there were lots of different interpretations of what people perceived as the rules of grammar, and I tried to distinguish between those rules that were clearly agreed upon, like the agreement of subject and verb, and those that weren't hard and fast, like the idea that you can't end a sentence with a preposition.

"But I am a big respecter of grammar. Writing all you want in whatever way you want tends to be a disease of the young. When writers can tell you all their feelings about a subject, but they haven't taken the time to master basic grammatical concepts and often haven't even mastered spelling and punctuation, I don't really take their arguments very seriously. I view that as an indication of the lack of rigor of their thinking. That's one of the great things about Strunk and White: I don't know that I'd agree with every one of their rules, but damn it, they had their rules, and they were pretty well agreed upon, and it makes it a lot easier for people to understand each other if they're following the same rules of communication. It's not as though you're restricted by these basic rules of writing that are intended to make your thoughts clearer. There's no rule I know of in Strunk and White that restricts you from expressing any thought you want to express. I'm sure there are times when a good writer will deliberately violate rules for effect. The rules of communication are rules that help people understand each other, but they don't restrict what you're thinking any more than you're restricted in communicating over the telephone just because both telephones have to operate on the same system in order to work. It's good, not bad, to have that kind of rule and structure."

Elmore Leonard is one of America's most prolific and successful novelists. Many of his books and stories have been turned into movies, including favorites such as *Out of Sight, Get Shorty, Be Cool, Jackie Brown* (from the book *Rum Punch*), and *3:10 to Yuma*. Leonard is widely known and praised for the spareness of his prose style, his avoidance of pointless decoration, and a positively Strunkian focus on omitting needless words.

In 2007, Leonard published his own brief book of advice for writers, *Elmore Leonard's 10 Rules of Writing,* which, at just over one thousand words, makes Strunk and White look like windbags. It's a fun list of brief, slightly idiosyncratic pointers (Number 1: "Never open a book with weather") aimed primarily at fiction writers hoping to bring to their work some of the crackle and punch of Leonard's own fiction. Leonard says he had a copy of *The Elements of Style* on his shelf for years and used to consult it occasionally, though he seems now to have misplaced it. No matter; he's long had *Elements*' key points well in hand.

A cardinal rule of Leonard's style is an assiduous effort to keep himself out of his own works. "I'm mostly concerned with remaining invisible," he says. "I'm not in my books. I don't have the language to write what I would consider serious literature, the kind where the writers are confident of their voice and they're telling the story and there's no question about it. In my books, I'm not telling the story. They're always from the point of view of a character. So when I write, I try not to use words that I might normally use if the character whose point of view I'm writing from wouldn't know and use those words. And my characters, for the most part, are not very educated. But the reason my style developed the way it did is that I'm just not going to come off as a literary author. I don't have the language and I don't have that kind of interest in the language. I don't have an interest in *telling;* I'm more interested in showing what's going on. I want to keep it simple, and I don't want to use a lot of words; I try to be as spare in that regard as I can."

In *The Elements of Style,* Chapter V, Rule 5, E. B. White says, "Revising is part of writing." Leonard agrees, but takes it a step further. "Writing *is* rewriting," he says, but unlike many writers who use the revision process to shake out the excess and streamline their prose, Leonard finds that his stories tend to expand during this phase. "I rewrite all the time," he says. "I'll get three or four pages one day, then the next day I'll go over it and, more often than not, I'm adding rather than cutting, but still keeping it simple. It already *is* simple, but I'm adding things—a cigarette or a drink or something like that. That's important for pauses, stops. It's important for the rhythm of what I'm writing. It can't just be a whole page of back-and-forth, back-and-forth, two people talking. Well, that happens once in a while. But there have to be other words put in—maybe the way he notices what she's doing with her hair, or something like that, that gives it just enough of a pause so that there's a rhythm to it. I'm very, very aware of rhythm. I don't do a lot of cutting, but I'm rewriting all the time."

The nonfiction writer and humorist **Ian Frazier** was hired as a staff writer at *The New Yorker* in 1974. His published collections of essays, humorous and otherwise, include *Dating Your Mom; Nobody Better, Better Than Nobody; Coyote v. Acme; The Fish's Eye; Gone to New York;* and *Lamentations of the Father.* His nonfiction books include *Great Plains, Family,* and *On the Rez.*

"There are some simple rules I keep in mind, such as not using the same word four times in a sentence. Or, when I write a humor piece, I try not to use any significant word more than once. If you do use a word more than once, you do it for a reason. So you find yourself looking to express things in a different way, and that means that you think more about what you want to express in the first place. I have probably thousands of rules that I don't even know what they are. Here's another one: If you're writing humor and you have a moment where you're going to write something disgusting (and I don't do that very often), it should be as funny as it is disgusting. If it's really disgusting and not that funny, don't do it. Not that it comes up that much in my work. And it doesn't have to be in a written piece—you could hear it on TV, for instance, and you realize it's not as funny as the liberty it's taking with you would seem to justify. I think that the higher you strive, the higher expression you strive for, the better.

"Writing is a skill like carpentry. You have to know how to make the thing work. Somebody has to read it and know what the hell you're talking about. When my kids were in school, they had a kind of spelling called 'kids' spelling.' They were taught to just get it out there, it doesn't matter what the spelling is like— the point being that they didn't want to discourage expression or stop the kids just because they didn't know how to spell a word. I think that was an error. The rules contribute to what you say, including the rules of spelling and grammar and punctuation. I don't think they can be dispensed with. Of course expression takes many different forms, so I guess you can't say this is an *absolute* rule, but it's really important. And if you want to have a set of rules, if you accept that you should, then *The Elements of Style* is a very good place to start. They are good things to keep in mind, and to remind yourself of. This is what we're always striving for. It's not a straitjacket, it's not a prescription, but it's something that, when you fall real short of it, you know you're not writing that well."

Nicholson Baker is a novelist and nonfiction writer. His articles and reviews have appeared in *The New Yorker, The New York Review of Books, The Atlantic Monthly, The London Review of Books,* and elsewhere. His novels include *The Mezzanine, Vox, A Box of Matches,* and *The Anthologist.* His nonfiction books include *U and I, Double Fold,* and *Human Smoke.*

"One of the things that helped me learn to write was to copy out things that I loved. I had a commonplace book and I would actually handwrite—I still do, sometimes—passages that I think are interesting or that use a particular construction in a new way or in a way I hadn't encountered. That's not a rule so much as a way of practicing, but it allows the more complicated rules that are connected to the way you hear sentences to kind of float in without you having to think about parts of speech and that kind of thing. So that helped me a lot. The rules that I use have changed. I like things to sound spoken. Now when I write, I tend to shed adjectives that, in the past, I would have put in, that would have been interesting curlicues.

"The thing is, as you get older, you get simpler. We're all working toward that Strunk-in-the-sky ideal, but it takes us a while to get there. It's also true that the brain just changes what you're interested in; what pleases you changes, and your sense of what is funny and what's playful and the right way to say things that are true. All those things change, and you become impatient of certain things that you once thought were amazingly impressive; all that changes. Although sometimes the urge to be baroque comes rushing back, you know? In my book *U and I,* I said something about how the lyrical impulse goes as you get older and what you're hoping is that it will be replaced by a finer social attunedness or something. I'm just waiting. But lyricism is a beautiful thing, and it's really a young thing. And E. B. White himself—we shouldn't forget that he wrote poetry and I think probably had a few ambitions in that line. And his *Harper's* essays are, I think, lyrical. But there's a sinewiness there and a strength, an observed core of specificity that makes them great. And those 'Notes and Comment' pieces—they're sort of like little walnuts, you know? They're just tremendous little pieces. When I think of Strunk and White, because White is a practitioner and Strunk was a teacher, I feel that I want to listen more closely to what White says. So you're hearing that in me, that's all."

Adam Gopnik has written for *The New Yorker* since 1986, is a three-time winner of the National Magazine Award for Essay and Criticism, and won the George Polk Award for Magazine Reporting. He is the author of the best-selling *Paris to the Moon;* a novel for children, *The King in the Window; Through the Children's Gate;* and *Angels and Ages.* He is also the editor of *Americans in Paris: A Literary Anthology.* Gopnik was raised by professors; his mother is a linguist, and his father teaches English. An admirer of E. B. White since childhood, he describes his feelings about *The Elements of Style* as "a complicated ambivalence."

"I was educated enough by my parents to know that the Strunk stuff is based on a fallacy—the idea that there's an inherently right way to use *that* and an inherently wrong way to use *which,* and so on. Anybody who studies language knows that's just not true. The old battle—to be a little absolutist about it—the old battle between prescriptivists and naturalists isn't really a battle. The naturalists are right; language changes all the time, and language's rules change all the time. But having said that, I was struck by, and learned an enormous amount from, the section that White wrote at the end, 'An Approach to Style.' I was impressed by those pages because everything he said there seemed to me to make sense—not as some kind of absolute natural rule for the way writing should be, but as a kind of primer on how you would write the kind of writing I admired.

"Strunk's injunctions are sort of standard grammarians' injunctions from the turn of the last century, but done in a much more vivid and entertaining way than they're usually done. They're very much like what you find in *Fowler* and so on. I don't disagree with many of the things that it says, but some of it seems to me a little bit schoolmarmish. Like when people argue about the proper use of *hopefully*. The fact is, *hopefully* has simply changed its meaning over the last fifty years. It used to mean 'to be done with hope.' Now it's just an adverb meaning 'I hope that.' And it's silly to say there's a right way to use it or a wrong way. It has just changed its meaning, in the way that words like *terrible* and *artificial* and *awful* have changed their meanings. *Artificial* and *awful* were once words that you used in praise, meaning 'full of artifice' and 'inspiring awe.' Now they're pejoratives. Words just change their meanings sometimes. So I don't have a lot of time for that side of it. But I do think that the struggle for clarity, the struggle for transparency, the struggle for simplicity are all very important for writing.

"I think this is a terribly important point, and some people have a hard time grasping it: You don't have to believe that the practices White believed in are natural rules—are absolute hard-and-fast injunctions—in order to choose to write that way. It's like marriage: You don't have to believe that marriage is a natural, sacred institution in order to be completely monogamous. You do it because you happen to value it yourself. I've spent the last twenty-some years of my life devoted to *New Yorker* style. And when I have a piece in the works, I spend a lot of time working with Ann Goldstein. She's the magazine's genius of style. Ann and I spend literally hours arguing about and debating semicolons, *that*s and *which*es, beginning sentences with *and,* paragraph breaks, all of the details of that kind of stylistic obsession—the things that Strunk and White deal with in *The Elements of Style*. But I don't think that we do it because there's a rule that says that's the one right way to write. We do it because we have a certain idea about style in our heads. We have a certain tone, a certain voice that we're struggling to get to and that those rules help us express. In other words, I love that style. I love that voice, and I struggle to achieve it to the degree that I can. But I don't have the illusion that it's a set of rules that are naturally generated or that everyone need follow.

"One reason for my ambivalence is that there are many kinds of wonderful writing that don't conform to the rules in *The Elements of Style*. Dr. Johnson's writing is full of ten-cent words and very complicated Latinate constructions, and Dr. Johnson is a better writer than Strunk ever was—maybe even a better writer than White. Herman Melville doesn't write that way. James Joyce doesn't write that way. Wallace Stevens doesn't write that way. Thomas Pynchon doesn't write that way. They are not bad writers; they're very good writers. And it's not just that you write in an exception for their genius. A writer has to find the tools that are right for him. What's the greatest American novel, after all? In my mind, it's *Huck Finn*. *Huck Finn* is written in dialect; it's written in 'bad English.' And so is *The Catcher in the Rye*.

"I think White would have recognized all this and accepted it emphatically. He knew all of that. I think that once you've set *The Elements of Style* up as a standard, as a guide or set of rules, then you appropriately rebel against it. If you understand it as a helpful book of advice toward achieving a certain kind of writing, which is a useful kind of writing—clear, simple, lucid writing—then I think it's very valuable. There are no rules for good writing. Good writing comes in as many different styles and flavors as there are good writers. At the same time, the kind of writing I do myself, the kind of writing I believe in, does have for its values a certain kind of clarity, lucidity, wit, bounce, and transparency. So maybe the best way to say this is *The Elements of Style* is a very good guide to writing the kind of prose that it's a very good guide to writing."

3

A Squeaky Voice
from the Past

Some of its charm and value for me unquestionably
derives from my memory of the man himself.

—E. B. WHITE

When the 1918 edition of *The Elements of Style* landed on
E. B. White's desk at *The New Yorker* in March 1957, his
memory of the book was hazy. It had been sent by a classmate
and friend, Howard Stevenson, editor of the *Cornell Alumni
News*. The previous summer, when the Stevensons visited the
Whites on their farm in Maine, the men had reminisced about
Strunk, and Stevenson had made a mental note to dig up a copy
of the professor's thumbnail credo and send it White's way. He
had finally succeeded in unearthing, from the university library,
a copy that had been deposited there by Strunk himself, and the
library staff was pleased to let Stevenson pass it along to White,
who, at that point, was one of Cornell's most well-known alumni.

Stevenson's gift, the book White held in his hand, was a wisp of a thing, more along the lines of a pamphlet, the approximate size of the instructions for your digital camera or a brochure presented to you by your dentist, a perky tract about flossing or gum disease. Five inches wide and seven inches tall, it was forty-three pages long and saddle-stitched—that is, held together by two wire staples crimped through the book's spine. The cover was lightly textured card stock, gray-tan with a narrow navy stripe running top to bottom at the spine, front and back. The cover design was a clean graphic implementation of the Strunkian aesthetic, a simple key-lined box surrounding only the essentials:

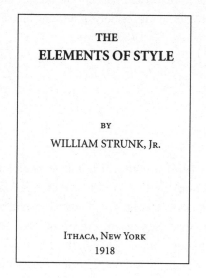

THE
ELEMENTS OF STYLE

BY

WILLIAM STRUNK, Jr.

ITHACA, NEW YORK
1918

The booklet had been privately printed, according to the small type near the bottom of the copyright page, by the Press of W. P. Humphrey, Geneva, N.Y.

White was charmed by the gift and by the memories it evoked of his old professor, who had died eleven years before Stevenson's gift arrived. Almost immediately, White began plans to

E. B. White, in his office at
The New Yorker
Used by permission of Allene White and
the estate of E. B. White.

write an admiring piece about Will Strunk and *The Elements of Style* for *The New Yorker*. But while his memory of Strunk was clear enough, White's recall of the "little book" was blurred by time (for example, he mistakenly recalled the class as English 20; it was English 8). He wrote back to Stevenson in early April, thanking him for the copy of *Elements* and asking for help in remembering some details.

25 West 43

2 April 1957

Dear Steve:

    I was overwhelmed to get the little book, filched from the library, and I hope I deserve it. Last night I went through it, seeing

*Will in every word and phrase and line—in Charles's friend, in
Burns's poems, in the comma after each term except the last. What
a book, what a man! Will so loved the clear, the brief, the bold—
and his book is clear, brief, bold.*

*It may be that I'll try to do a piece on "The Elements of Style"
for The New Yorker. Perhaps you can fill me in on a few matters
on which I am vague or uninformed (My memory is poor and
needs jolting). Do you recall the name of the course known as
English 20? Was it called "English usage and style"? Was the "little
book" on sale at bookstores in Ithaca, and were students in English
20 asked to buy the book? The title page says "Privately Printed,
Ithaca, N. Y., 1918" and overleaf there is the mark of the "Press
of W. P. Humphrey, Geneva, N. Y." Would this mean that Will
paid the bill for getting out the book, or would the University have
picked up the tab? I am, as you see, ignorant on such matters. Do
you know whether the book was used in colleges and universities
other than Cornell? I take it no use is made of it by the English
Department in this day and age; it would be considered too
arbitrary, too cocky, too short. ("Omit needless words. Vigorous
writing is concise.") Did you come out of English 20 owning a copy
of the little book? Do you still have your copy? For some reason
that escapes me, I think I never had a copy of the book, even when
I was a student in the course. I could be wrong about this, but I
seem to remember being somewhat baffled (at first) by frequent
references to "the little book", not knowing what the "little book"
was. Even now, I am not certain whether these pages come back
to me as pages that I studied, or whether I simply remember
the contents as they were reproduced in class by Will himself,
who must have followed the book pretty closely. ("Make definite
assertions.")*

*If you can answer, and feel like answering, any of these tedious
questions, I would be delighted to hear from you. Hell, I would be*

delighted to hear from you anyway. ("The lefthand version gives
the impression that the writer is undecided or timid; he seems
unable or afraid to choose one form of expression and hold
to it.")

Was Will of German descent? The name Strunk sounds
German. Is Mrs. Strunk alive? Sis? Oliver? Another boy? And
do you remember what year it was that Will died—or a rough
approximation? Do you know whether English 20 was a freshman
course? I don't remember whether I took it as a freshman,
sophomore, junior, or senior, but I think I took it early in my
college years.

Thanks again, Steve, for this gift. This is a late day (I almost
said a "very" late day, but Will hated "very") for me to meet
up with "The Elements of Style" by William Strunk, Jr. I shall
treasure the book as long as there are any elements of life in my
bones. Hope you and Mildred will get to Maine again. If you do,
you will get fed, not merely ginned; and I will put you in my
18-foot sloop and whirl you round and round. ("Place the
emphatic words of a sentence at the end.")

> *Yrs gratefully,*
> *Andy*

White's essay about Strunk appeared in the July 27, 1957, issue
of *The New Yorker,* under the heading "Letter from the East."
The Strunk reminiscence is sandwiched between two largely un-
related sections of the "Letter"; the first is about White's battles
with mosquitoes in his Turtle Bay apartment, the last a rueful
warning about the mismanagement of radioactive waste. The
mosquito piece moves, in its final paragraph, to the question of
trimming the excess from one's life. The Whites were then in the
midst of packing up their affairs in New York and preparing to

quit their apartment and move full-time to the farm in Maine. "Every so often I make an attempt to simplify my life," White wrote, "burning my books behind me, selling the occasional chair, discarding the accumulated miscellany." One of the books he had decided to neither burn nor leave behind was "a small one that arrived in the mail not long ago, a gift from a friend in Ithaca." White then introduced the world to William Strunk and *The Elements of Style*.

"It was known on the campus in my day as 'the little book,'" he wrote, "with the stress on the word 'little.'" *Elements*, White said, had been Strunk's attempt to gather the principles of good writing "on the head of a pin," and he drew a lively verbal portrait of Strunk, who emerged as archetypically professorial—blinking at his charges from behind round, steel-rimmed spectacles, holding his lapels and leaning over his desk to deliver his positive, if sometimes eccentric, style-related pronouncements in loud, confident tones. The essay made clear White's admiration for Strunk's qualities as a teacher and a man, and his respect for Strunk's devotion to the principles of style he preached. "I treasure *The Elements of Style* for its sharp advice," White wrote, "but I treasure it even more for the audacity and self-confidence of its author. Will knew where he stood." By the end of the essay, readers were cheering along with White for the memory of Strunk, admiring and maybe a little envious of the professor's certainty, of his fervor for intellectual and moral clarity in a world gone soft. In that issue of *The New Yorker*, the "Letter from the East" is long, its columns thinly threaded through a gauntlet of advertisers targeting the magazine's affluent, culture-conscious readers, making for a wry contrast with White's meditations on simplicity and Strunk's admonitions about bunk: Abercrombie & Fitch, Ballantine's Scotch, Cadillac ("Without a Word Being Spoken . . . a new Cadillac car states the case for its owner with remarkable clarity and eloquence"), United Airlines (touting the juicy steaks on their *for-men-only* "Executive" flights from New York to Chicago), and a full-page spread of a leggy knockout in capri pants enjoying a Pabst Blue Ribbon beer with her man.

Dear Mr. _____

Thanks for letting me know that the little book gets around. It not only got to Japan, the Japanese now have it in translation. I can't imagine how that would help anyone, but I own a copy of the book and am always delighted with the mysterious east.

Sincerely,
E. B. White

The same week the essay was published, White was contacted by Jack Case, an editor at the Macmillan Company, who told White that if *The Elements of Style* was everything White had made it out to be, Macmillan might be interested in republishing it. Case and his boss, the assistant director of the company's college department, Harry Cloudman, felt the book's unique, somewhat eccentric qualities were just what the market was crying out for, as Case made clear in a letter pitching to White the idea of their republishing the book, using White's *New Yorker* essay as its introduction, before anyone at Macmillan had even laid eyes on *The Elements of Style*.

July 26, 1957

Dear Mr. White:

What we would do with Professor Strunk's book is reset it in an appropriate type face, large enough to be pleasantly legible, print it on good paper, and put it in an attractive binding, probably a combination of cloth and paper over boards. The trade edition, if there were one, would have a jacket; the college edition would not. We have not yet consulted our trade department on this, and our interest in the project is independent of any that they might have. We think that if the various business details could be settled early in the fall we could publish the book sometime in the spring.

Those are the bare outlines. The use of your essay as a preface to the book would be crucial. You might want to change the first sentence, lest some freshman conclude that your usual practice with books is to burn them; the rest, through the third "Get the little book!" would stand. The textbooks of 1918 are not easily refloated. We think that, amidst the crazy currents now running every which way in freshman English, your essay could draw up a tide that would get this off the beach. Probably you do not know how much your work and your opinions are admired and respected by college teachers of English. The same admiration and respect, and a confidence in the power of your influence to get attention for what you think is worth it, has moved us here today to excitement over a publishing project which, under other auspices, would be regarded as hopeless.

We are not underrating the college teacher. We do not expect him to ask his students to buy this book because E. B. White says it is good. We do expect that what you say will open the teacher's eyes to the excellence of the book, so that as he examines it he will find himself of your opinion. Certainly this will not be true of all teachers. We think it will be true of enough.

All this is, of course, before we have read Professor Strunk's work. We may beat a retreat later. We shall all be surprised if this happens. . . .

We don't embark on many college book projects in a mood in which enthusiasm is a principal ingredient, and a good thing, too! But we think our instinct is right on this one. Now please let us see the little book in the cold light of Monday morning if you can get it here that soon. Naturally we shall be most interested in knowing your reaction to the idea.

Sincerely yours,
J. G. Case

White heard from others, too, Strunks among them. Will's son Oliver, by that time well embarked on his own teaching career at Princeton, wrote to thank White for the touching tribute to his father. Oliver was particularly pleased by the glimpse that White's essay had given him of Will Jr. at work, since the Strunk children had never been allowed in their father's classroom. White also heard from fellow Cornellians who were grateful to see Strunk memorialized in this way. One, an antiquarian bookseller in Ithaca, wrote to White in November and said that his phone had started ringing eighteen hours after the *New Yorker* essay on Strunk had appeared and had been ringing "ever since"—White's readers were seeking out any existing copies of *The Elements of Style.*

NICHOLSON BAKER

What I love about the book is that it's kind of an act of affection toward a former professor. E. B. White didn't republish the book because he wanted it to be canonical or required reading or some kind of rite of passage. He just felt that these were some useful, well-expressed, simple rules that had helped him a great deal when he was a student and that he could add on something—this sort of frothy, beautiful thing of a chapter that blesses the rules and then says, of course, you have to have more. If the book is treated as though it's graven in stone, that's a mistake. If it's cited with too much grim authority, it becomes something that you rebel against. But I haven't felt that way about it, and I think it's just because it's not meant to be a magnum opus. It's a quiet word to the wise. There's a humility to the way he presents it that's very appealing to me.

In late July 1957, White mailed his only copy of *The Elements of Style*—the copy Stevenson had sent from the Cornell library—to Jack Case at Macmillan.

July 29, 1957

Dear Mr. Case:

Thanks for your letter.

I'm enclosing my copy of "The Elements of Style." You can see at a glance that Professor Strunk omitted needless words. Whether the book has other virtues that would recommend it to teachers of English, I don't feel qualified to say. Some of its charm and value for me unquestionably derives from my memory of the man himself— his peculiar delivery of these rules of usage and the importance with which he managed to invest the subject. Sometimes the book, like the man, seems needlessly compressed, and it is undeniably notional. On the other hand, it contains several short essays that are gems; they still tickle me. My guess is that Will Strunk had a particular reason for writing this handbook: I think he felt the need of a labor-saving device in correcting papers. With the "little book" in the hands of his students, he could simply write in the margin of a theme: "See Rule 2."

Should you decide that you want to re-issue the book, I would feel justified in giving Macmillan permission to use my piece only if I was satisfied that the Strunk heirs were happy about the project. Professor Strunk's widow is alive, I believe—living at 380 Crown Street, Meriden, Conn. There is a son Oliver Strunk who is on the Princeton faculty, 80 College Avenue. And there is another son Edwin, with the Chrysler Corporation. He lives at 1594 Penistone Road, Birmingham, Mich. Whether the copyright is in effect or not, I would expect you to get permission from the estate and pay royalties to the estate.

As for me, I think I should receive a share of the royalties, and I'd like your suggestion as to what sort of division you would think fair to all concerned. The New Yorker, incidentally, doesn't enter the picture—it does not take any reprint money. Never has. The contributor gets all. (It's a very lovable old weekly.) See page 40 of the little book—use of the word "very."

As for my essay, I'm quite willing to fix the first sentence (burn fewer books). I am also willing to do whatever I can to make the piece useful and suitable as an introduction. I may even have a bit more to say on the subject of rhetoric, now that I am suddenly faced with this unexpected audience.

I'm leaving for Maine on Wednesday night. My address there is North Brooklin. Please take good care of "The Elements of Style."

Sincerely,
E. B. White

Before the deal could be completed, the matter of copyright had to be considered. *The Elements of Style* had been revised and republished several times since the original 1918 edition, and it had been a Harcourt, Brace publication since 1920. The last version, published in 1935, had been revised by another Cornell instructor, Edward A. Tenney, and released as *The Elements and Practice of Composition,* with a section of exercises added to the back of the book. It took Case and Cloudman nearly a year, from the summer of 1957 to the spring of 1958, to sort out the copyright status of the various editions. The Strunks, Emilie and her son Oliver, the executor of his father's estate, were happy to see the project move forward, and Oliver was helpful early on in Macmillan's efforts to identify the various editions and investigate any existing copyright claims. In May 1958, Case wrote to White to let him know they had finally established that the rights were free and clear, that nothing stood in the way of copyrighting a new edition of *The Elements of Style* with White as coauthor. Macmillan was ready to offer a contract, with the royalties split fifty-fifty between White and the Strunk estate. Case went on:

> We should, of course, want the New Yorker *piece, changed or unchanged, with or without additions, as an introduction. In this, or outside it, I think the latter, there should be something that would serve as a preface to this edition, a brief account of what has been done and why.*
>
> *We now believe that unless THE ELEMENTS OF STYLE were to be reissued simply as a kindly memorial to its author rather than as a useful book for the second half of the century, certain editorial changes would have to be made, and that you are the person to make them. I think you will at once feel a reluctance to lay violent hands upon something that was once well done. Actually what we should ask would not amount to this.*

First there are certain omissions to make, simply because some references are no longer useful or especially significant. . . .

We have thought that it might interest you to tinker a bit with the usage section, possibly adding some currently troublesome items. . . .

We don't think that the various suggestions quite add up to a revision of Professor Strunk's book, to actual rewriting, or to deletion and substitution that he would not himself want to make if he were here to do so, except with regard to two or three crotchety passages based on excessively personal aversions. We should like to have you saw off bits of outdated scroll work here and there, and then build onto the sound essential structure some advice of your own about the elements of good writing. Just where the joints would come and how they would be made could be worked out later; first we should like you to form your own picture of the dimensions of the remodeling to be done. . . .

Sincerely yours,
J. G. Case

With a clear road before him, White threw himself into the job. Far beyond simply adding his reworked *New Yorker* essay to the book, he committed to a thorough edit of Strunk's original text and the contribution of a new chapter on writing—the "bit more" he had mentioned "on the subject of rhetoric." At the start of the project, Case sent White a photostat copy of Strunk's edition, with the pages pasted onto individual sheets of typing paper, for White to mark up with his changes. White eventually found it an impractical way to proceed and ended up retyping most of the book from scratch, revising as he went. By late fall of 1958, he had almost finished his work, and he sent Case a status report, in response to the editor's request for some specifics required by Macmillan's marketing department.

November 3, 1958

Dear Mr. Case:

For the guidance of your catalogue writer, here is the way the book stands.

I have tinkered the Strunk text—have added a bit, subtracted a bit, rearranged it in a few places, and in general have made small alterations that seemed useful and in the spirit of Strunk. The first two sections of the "Composition" chapter sustained the heaviest attack; I felt that they were narrow and bewildering. (In their new form they are merely bewildering.)

I have added a number of entries in the "Words and Expressions Commonly Misused" chapter, and as a result that chapter will run longer. In the main, though, the "little" book will end up very nearly the same size as the original: it will still be small, concise, opinionated, non-comprehensive—a squeaky voice from the past.

My New Yorker *piece, I think, should go unchanged (except for the lead sentence) as a preface. I shall write a short note, or foreword, explaining the circumstances that brought the book back into print and telling roughly what has taken place.*

I am dropping Chapter VI, "Words Often Misspelled." In its place will appear a chapter by me, called (tentatively) "An Approach to Style." Here I drop a few cautionary, and I fear paternalistic, hints; I discuss style in its broader meaning—not style in the sense of what is correct but style in the sense of what is distinguished and distinguishing. The foreword will make clear that this chapter is my work, not Strunk's, and that my professor might, if alive, heartily disapprove of every word of it.

*This essay on Style—Chapter VI in the book—runs around
3500 words, I would guess. I have been letting it stand, to see if
some of the lumps and other impurities would settle, and I hope to
improve it before I have done. In writing it, I deliberately departed
from the strict rhetorical face of style, in an attempt to give the
little book an extra dimension, which, considering what is taking
place, it can probably use. In short, I shall have a word or two to
say about attitudes in writing: the why, the how, the beartraps, the
power, and the glory.*

*I am in New York this week and will be returning home to
Maine on the 11th if my wife is able to travel by then. I'm taking
the book back with me for the final go-around and to give it the
inestimable advantage of coming under her editorial eye. She is a
better grammarian, organizer, teacher, editor, and mother than I
am, and has saved an untold number of lives.*

Yours sincerely,
E. B. White

White posted the complete manuscript to Jack Case three days
before Thanksgiving Day.

24 November 1958

Dear Mr. Case:

*The book goes off by registered mail today, in three envelopes—
one, two, three. I hope it reaches you before you sit down to your
turkey. My chapter on style runs long, but I let myself go, being a
white-haired old man, mumbling in my corner.*

*The manuscript pages are numbered—front stuff in red
numerals, main stuff in blue numerals. Throughout the book
I have indicated, by red lines, the parts that will presumably*

be set in small type. Strunk's rules are numbered, 1 to 18. My commandments in Chapter VI, which I call "reminders", are numbered, 1 to 21. It may be that you will want to dream up some typographical distinction between these two sets of numbers, for ease in reference. But I guess it's clear enough what is taking place.

You will probably be surprised to see that so much of the material is in the form of typescript, instead of the pasted pages of type that you provided me with. I started out working with these pages, but got nowhere. For one thing, they were the revised edition, not the original, and this became unbearably confusing; I was trying to shoot a deer by aiming at a rabbit. Only when I shoved a piece of yellow paper into a typewriter did I begin to make progress.

I've done nothing about permissions. I quote Wolfe, Faulkner, Hemingway, Cather, Frost, Whitman. All except the Cather are, I think, fair use. Will your office square this stuff, or do you count on me to do it? The sources are:

Wolfe—"Look Homeward Angel"
Faulkner—"The Hamlet"
Hemingway—"The Undefeated"
Cather—"My Antonia"
Frost—"Stopping by Woods"
Whitman—"I Sing the Body Electric"

I have written "A Note on This Book", to run first, explaining what happened. If this does not say what you think is needed in that spot, I shall of course be happy to try again.

In general I am pleased with the way things have worked out, although I'm so punchy at the moment I do not trust my eyes. The word list, I think, has been improved. The final entry, by the way, is one I particularly like because I didn't write it—my wife did. The business about "would" and getting from the general to

*the particular. She tells me that the commonest derangement in
the body of fiction manuscripts received at the New Yorker is the
lack of transition from the general to the particular. So she threw
herself into the word "would" with a happy cry.*

   *I'll be very glad to have your estimate of my remarks on style.
Do they fit this book, or are they out of place in a Strunk murder?
You may shoot at them with anything from a gum eraser to a
poisoned arrow; the only thing I can't stand is to have my feelings
spared, or an editor failing to say what is on his mind.*

                              Sincerely,
                              E. B. White

*P.S. I have no copy of my piece, or of anything else, so if you lose it,
lose it good and we can all just relax.*

Sixteen months after first learning of Strunk and *The Elements
of Style,* Case and Cloudman were ecstatic to finally have White's
completed manuscript in hand. Case wrote back to White, gid-
dily: "It has arrived. It looks fine. Harry Cloudman and I are
going to smudge it up with cranberry sauce at my house tomorrow. . . . Congratulations on hitting your deadline right on the
nose!"

   White's tinkering had been thorough. He had freshened every
chapter without fudging either the spirit or, in most cases, the
letter of Strunk's law. The "narrow and bewildering" sections
that White had noted in the chapter on composition had been
Strunk's Rules 9 and 10, concerning the organization of essays
and paragraphs. In an uncharacteristically garrulous treatment,
Strunk had directed his remarks specifically to students writing critical essays on literature and offered several structural
templates for theme development that no doubt struck White as
unnecessarily confining.

A report on a poem, written for a class in literature, might consist of seven paragraphs:

A. Facts of composition and publication.
B. Kind of poem; metrical form.
C. Subject.
D. Treatment of subject.
E. For what chiefly remarkable.
F. Wherein characteristic of the writer.
G. Relationship to other works.

The contents of paragraphs C and D would vary with the poem. Usually, paragraph C would indicate the actual or imagined circumstances of the poem (the situation), if these call for explanation, and would then state the subject and outline its development. If the poem is a narrative in the third person throughout, paragraph C need contain no more than a concise summary of the action. Paragraph D would indicate the leading ideas and show how they are made prominent, or would indicate what points in the narrative are chiefly emphasized.

Strunk's instructions on paragraph development went on to include a page and a half of closely parsed and numbered examples. White's rewrite of Rules 9 and 10 removed the lit-crit specifics and Strunk's nearly mathematical analysis. White broadened and simplified the discussion, reshaping it into a livelier, friendlier consideration of the writer's purposes and the reader's needs.

White's changes to what had been Strunk's fifth chapter, "Words and Expressions Commonly Misused," almost doubled the page count of that chapter, even after he deleted seven of

Strunk's original entries, including *dependable* ("A needless substitute for *reliable, trustworthy*"); *lose out* ("Meant to be more emphatic than *lose,* but actually less so, because of its commonness"); *one hundred and one* ("Retain the *and* in this and similar expressions, in accordance with the unvarying usage of English prose from Old English times"); and *viewpoint* ("Write *point of view,* but do not misuse this, as many do, for *view* or *opinion*"). After removing Strunk's outdated peeves, White added forty-nine new entries to the chapter: *aforesaid, allude, allusion, and/or, anybody, anyone, at, but, can, can't hardly, comprise, contact, data, different than, disinterested, divided into, don't, enormity, enthuse, farther-further, folk, get, illusion, imply-infer, inside of—inside, interesting, in the last analysis, irregardless, lay, leave, like, loan, me, none, participle for verbal noun, personalize, personally, prove, refer, shall-will, should, split infinitive, that-which, the foreseeable future, tortuous-torturous, transpire, type, unique, -wise.*

White's greatest achievement in the refurbished *Elements of Style* was his Chapter V, "An Approach to Style." The essay has come down to us as one of the most lucid and illuminating representations we have of a writer's process of creation. If Strunk had laid down the rules, White's Chapter V was about life on the other side of the rules—a potent distillation of theory and practice gleaned from his long career. But it had not come easily to him. Just three weeks before turning in the manuscript, he had written to his brother Stanley complaining that he was "completely bogged down" in the chapter. "Turns out," he wrote, "after about 50 years in the vineyard, that I have no ideas about what I have been doing, or why or how." Even as he turned it in, he was unsure whether he had in fact accomplished what he wanted to with the piece. White and his editor would return to Chapter V in later correspondence.

Dear Miss _____

A lot of grammarians should take up the snare-drums. Half way through my editing of the book, I came close to dropping the whole business and taking them up myself.

Incidentally, while I have you on the line, "alright" should be two words: all right.

Many thanks for your letter.

Sincerely,
E. B. White

After Jack Case and Harry Cloudman had read the manuscript closely, Case wrote an appreciative letter to White.

December 4, 1958

Dear Mr. White:

I have been plugging away at the manuscript almost continuously since it arrived, and so have not had a chance to tell you how much we like it. By Thanksgiving evening both Harry Cloudman and I had read all of it once and parts of it twice, and were quoting to each other sentence after sentence of the final chapter.

That is a fine thing, delightful and wise, as we knew it would be—from the fun about cats to the startling Wolfe quote, and your equally startling treatment of it, both of which would make a corpse sit bolt upright; from the gentle, firm counsel not to thrash about in the stream to the sharing of your hard-won glimpses of the mysterious heart of style. All this, and much more, is not only wonderfully good in itself; it fulfills our common purpose to make those matters of writing come alive for the reader who needs help, and to keep them as clear as may be. . . .

Sincerely,
J. G. Case

The typescript of the 1959 edition—a sizable stack of White's preferred yellow typing paper interleaved with corrections, inserts, taped-in sections from Strunk's original text, and instructions for typesetter and printer—is preserved in the White collection at Cornell. For an *Elements of Style* disciple, it is an inspiring sight, imparting something like the electric thrill of proximity to history I felt when leaning over the Magna Carta in the subdued lighting of the British Library. An artifact from the days of typewriters, colored-pencil corrections, and pasteup, a physical typescript is a reassuring thing to see and hold in this age when books routinely travel the complete route from author to printing press in the digital realm without materializing, corporeally speaking, until they emerge from the bindery. A typescript of the old style is a gloriously untidy stack of papers with the real-world presence of a created thing—a flapping, pasted, taped-up offspring born from toil, the living output of an artisan at work. In a manuscript that has been through an editorial round or two, a good portion of the process of authorial refinement is laid bare, and you can watch over the shoulders of author and editor as decisions are made, various lines of approach essayed and abandoned, thoughts and expression sharpened.

In the 1959 typescript, White's clean-typed pages, double-spaced pica, have been layered over with penciled printer instructions and editorial comment—indentations indicated, caps and itals duly underlined, typefaces and spacing between paragraphs called out in point sizes. Some penciled lines have been crossed out, some smudged out, some scratched over with pen and new words typed above; words, phrases, sentences, and whole paragraphs have been written in by hand and circled, with lines guiding them to their proper places in the text. Strips of paper have been glued in here and there with corrections, pasted over sections they're replacing. In places, whole pages from Strunk's original *Elements* have been taped in; they, too, are covered with editorial graffiti, the cellophane tape browning and brittle, some of its glue turned to dust. Some inserted pages are entirely hand-written, penciled in White's strong, sharp hand. White's *New Yorker* essay about Strunk, most of which is used as the book's introduction, has been clipped directly from the magazine's pages and pasted in strips onto two pages of white typing paper.

WILL BLYTHE

If Strunk and White's advice were transposed into advice for living, I think you'd end up with one of those kind of high-minded New Englanders, someone who cares about politics, who cares about truth and honesty. He would be very conscientious; he would have a slight tendency toward understatement, a wryness. He might occasionally wear a little bow-tie, but that would be about the extent of his ornamentation.

Will Blythe is the former fiction editor of *Esquire* and the author of *To Hate Like This Is to Be Happy Forever.*

Through the winter of 1958–59, *The Elements of Style* was put through its editorial paces at Macmillan and refined with a good deal of back-and-forth between New York and the farm in Maine. Jack Case gathered opinions from experts in the field, and White, as promised, sought the "inestimable advantage" of his wife's editorial opinion. Katharine's involvement in the enterprise was energetic and substantial, and she provided White with several sets of typed notes that addressed the expert critiques Case was collecting. During this period, Case was also lining up marketing efforts for the book, and to that end inquired whether White would be willing to make an appearance at an upcoming Macmillan sales conference and speak to the assembled sales force. White's reply was a characteristically droll refusal, and also a playful indication of how much the final cleanup of *Elements* was occupying his thoughts.

10 December 1958

Dear Mr. Case:

In answer to your request that I say a few words to the trade and college salesmen I'll have to acquaint you with the non-speechmaking side of me—almost the only facet that amounts to anything.

As for lunching with you at the Players', that I'd like.

All the stuff has arrived and I am at work on it. But mine is a strange existence, between barn and house. It is not always clear to me whether I am watering a calf or milking a strunk. But I do my best.

Sincerely,
E. B. White

In the letters between Case and White, it's clear that a friendship—a mutually admiring professional acquaintance, at least—was growing. By the time the book was ready for press, the two had been corresponding, and sweating the details of *Elements* together, for nearly two years. Case's letters had relaxed and become shaded with the sort of wry humor that White himself enjoyed. Case prized the relationship, and the easy rapport that had sprung up between them.

March 19, 1959

Dear Mr. White:

It may comfort you to know, during the nail-biting period between proof and publication, that yesterday both Miss Anderson and I read the foundry proof, and, except for one missing letter on the copyright page, could find no fault in it. While it would be miraculous if something somewhere did not get past us all, such as a misspelling of "White" or "Macmillan", I am almost persuaded that the miracle has occurred.

My reading did turn up two instances of "the above" that I had not spotted, or had failed to talk you out of, but I am content to regard them as beauty marks accentuating the loveliness of the whole. The entry,

Case. *Often unnecessary.*

makes me a little moody, but I can only say, "How true," and thank you for that considerate adverb.

I should be sick to death of reading this book. That I am not, that I continue to find new depths in such things as "creative writing is the Self escaping into the open," "the setting of a word is just as restrictive as the setting of a jewel," "the writer must sympathize with the reader's plight but never seek to know his

wants," confirms my belief that we were as right as we could be in
asking you to do this job, and makes me wish that Chapter V were
twenty times its length.

Sincerely,
J. G. Case

The Elements of Style (by William Strunk, Jr., With Revisions, an
Introduction, and a New Chapter on Writing, by E. B. White)
was published in late April 1959. Sales were good, and reviews in
the popular press were almost unanimously favorable. *The New
York Times*: "Buy it, study it, enjoy it. It's as timeless as a book
can be in our age of volubility." *The Boston Daily Globe*: "The Admirable Mr. E. B. White . . . has lately performed another public
service of the first magnitude." *The Cincinnati Enquirer*: "Anyone
who writes for public consumption would be doing himself and

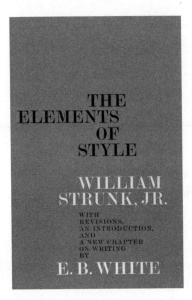

The Elements of Style, 1959
The Elements of Style *by William Strunk Jr. and*
E. B. White. Copyright by Pearson Education
Inc. Used by permission.

his readers a good service by reading over these pages at least once a month. There are only 71 of them." In a short review on White's home turf, *The New Yorker* noted that in its "brevity, clarity, and prickly good sense, it is, unlike most such manuals, a book as well as a tool. . . . His old teacher would have been proud of him."

Jack Case, Harry Cloudman, and company were ecstatic about its success. Case watched sales closely, reported the numbers to White when substantial orders came in, and alerted him when to watch the newspapers.

July 22, 1959

Dear Andy:

For the next two or three weeks, keep an eye on the best-seller lists in the Sunday TIMES and HERALD-TRIBUNE. The Trib's is expected to break first.

What's got into the American people?

Yours in awe,
Jack

"If I seem unduly wide-eyed at all the attention the book has been getting in the trade field," Case wrote to White near the end of 1959, "that is the condition of most of us in this department, unused as we are to having the general public make a fuss over books of ours, but I have noticed that the trade boys also are not nonchalant about this success."

When the book was published, William Strunk's widow, Emilie, was in her late eighties and living with her daughter, Catherine, in Connecticut. She sent a thank-you note to White on the occasion. "I think you and I make a great pair," she wrote, "especially with you doing all the work." Later that year, she sent a longer note.

September 15, 1959

Dear Andie:

I have been wanting to write to you for some time, but the heat has had me down, down, down. I am just beginning to feel like a human being, and not a roast of beef just out of the oven.

You have been so wonderfully good, and so helpful over "our book" or rather Will's book I am still dazed over its success! There has been very little for me to do, you and Mr. Cloudman have done all the work.

I wonder if you are staying at your farm in Maine! Will and I were always so interested and amused, in reading the stories about your farm. Maine sounds so cool and attractive. But I hope for the best as so far September has treated us fairly well.

I hear the breakfast bell ringing and the house smells of coffee! I think I had better get really busy.

Gratefully yours,
Emilie Strunk

After receiving her first royalty check, in January 1960, Emilie wrote to White once again.

Jan 20/60

Dear Andy—

Thank you for your note, and for your thoughtfulness about my royalties. I got them the first week of this month, and I was stunned. I feel I did very little to be paid so much. I do hope you got as much or more. You did plenty of work. . . .

Mr. Cloudman also wrote me a very nice letter.

I see that the little book is still on the NY Times best seller list, or was last Sunday.

Gratefully yours,
Emilie Strunk

Elements was a May 1959 selection of the Book-of-the-Month Club. By August, between Case's college-text printings and those of his colleagues supplying the general trade bookstores, there were 60,000 copies in print. By November the book was riding high on best-seller lists (third in *The New York Times* and *Time* magazine, second in the *Chicago Tribune,* first in *The Washington Post*). At the end of its first year of publication, *The Elements of Style* had sold an astonishing 200,000 copies.

MEMORY

It was thanks to the stirring of E. B. White's memory—thirty-eight-year-old impressions left by an influential teacher, his class, and his little book—that *The Elements of Style* eventually found its wider audience, and the book went on to shape the style sensibilities of generations of students and writers. As lasting as was the impression that Strunk made on White, the book they created has left an even stronger imprint on the American imagination over the past fifty years, with the result that many people who care and think about writing have clear memories of their first experiences with the book—a squeaky voice from our own collective past. I asked the writers interviewed for this book to talk about their early memories and impressions of *The Elements of Style*.

Nicholson Baker's first memories of *The Elements of Style* are, not surprisingly, colored by sensory detail: "I have a vivid memory of this little kind of yellow book that I got when I decided that I didn't know how to write. I went to an experimental high school that was very, very free-form. We didn't really have to be anywhere; we didn't have to read many books. They were nice people, but they really didn't teach anything. They didn't teach writing. I decided that I wanted to take some college courses because I wanted to learn about literature, and I went to the college bookstore and there in the English section in the intro to writing classes, I found *The Elements of Style*. There was something nice about the *elements* of style. It was like the periodic table or something. It looked difficult, but it was short. I liked the shortness of it. I also remember that the binding was kind of tight, so that the book seemed to want to stay closed. I thought that was interesting. I actually didn't look into it carefully at first, partly because it seemed happier being shut. Also, I disagreed with some of it, which is what I think the book is all about. I had and still have an urge to use ornate words and have things really be complicated and glowing out from the shadows, and all sorts of things that it doesn't seem to me that Professor Strunk would have responded well to. But I dipped into it. And it helped me. I wouldn't say I learned to write using it, but it was just helpful to have a few bits of advice about what not to do. For instance, not to use, say, *irregardless.* That's one of the few things I remember. I remember reading the rule about how you weren't supposed to use *irregardless* and thinking, *Well, I've never heard anyone use* irregardless, *and I can't imagine why there would need to be a rule saying don't use that.* But that was part of what was fascinating about the book, actually—it was a book that was in some ways connected to a time that had passed, in that some of the slang words and mistakes, to me, sounded like old movies. But I kind of liked that.

"I then finally read E. B. White's contribution, the fifth chapter, and I read these four words: *a matter of ear.* That was what really hit me. Sure, rules are important, and White was obviously very struck by the certainty and the conviction that Strunk had, and it helped him, as it helps everybody to keep in mind things that you should do and shouldn't do—but when it comes right down to it, the next step is a matter of ear. So those four words were really the surviving bit of wisdom that I took away from the book. And I think, in some ways, that E. B. White's life is in reaction to Strunk, because he so effortlessly kind of dances around the rules so well that it's almost as if he's making fun of them a little bit."

Damon Lindelof is cocreator, executive producer, and head writer for *Lost,* one of television's most celebrated and addictive dramatic series. His essays have appeared in *The New York Times* and elsewhere, and he is the writer of the comic-book miniseries *Ultimate Wolverine vs. Hulk,* published by Marvel comics.

"My father was a big aficionado of Strunk and White and always had a copy handy. He was a bank executive, but in his spare time he was a writer, and he wrote essays and short stories and screenplays, a lot of which I didn't discover until after he passed on. He gave me a copy of *The Elements of Style* on, I think, at least two or three separate occasions. I think he would read my writing and realize that I was obviously not reading Strunk and White, so it would sort of turn up on Christmas, stuffed into a stocking, or he'd give it to me on my birthday, saying, 'This is great; you should read it. It will teach you how to write properly.' I would always kind of thumb through it, but it felt like it was a little too restrictive to me. And then, Stephen King, my favorite author, published his book *On Writing,* which is a combination of memoir and writing instruction. In that book, King praised Strunk and White to the moon and beyond, so I finally sat down and read through *The Elements of Style,* and I promised myself that if I were ever to do any real writing, that is, outside of the television/movie business, that I would employ it so that I wouldn't embarrass myself.

"One thing from *Elements* that has stuck with me is the phrase 'omit needless words.' Why use fifteen words when four words will do? That's the thing that really struck me. And now, when I look over some of the creative writing I did in college, I can barely get through it; it's so unnecessarily and egregiously verbose."

Frank McCourt was awarded the Pulitzer Prize for *Angela's Ashes,* his 1996 memoir about growing up poor in the lanes of Limerick, Ireland. Two subsequent books continued the story of his life: *'Tis* begins with McCourt's arrival in America at age nineteen. *Teacher Man* is the story of his thirty-year career as a schoolteacher in New York City.

"I was teaching in the Lower East Side, Seward Park High School, and in the corner of the book room there was a stack of dust-laden books—dusty and untouched by human hands. They were copies of *The Elements of Style* that had been ordered by the head of the English Department, who was a very scholarly man. He thought we could use it, but the English teachers took a look at it and shied away, because this was the age of descriptive grammar rather than prescriptive. But I started reading it, and I was intrigued, mainly by E. B. White's introduction. That's what got me—there was something about it. It was delicious. So there was this stack of books there in the book room, and I tried to use them, but for the kind of kids I had at Seward Park High School, many of them wrestling with English as a second language, that went nowhere. They didn't need that. It was too frightening, because Mr. Strunk approached grammar with a club. He laid down the law. But it was good for me because I didn't know anything about grammar. The only grammar I knew was what I got in school in Ireland, and that was Irish grammar, which is beyond anybody's comprehension."

As much as anything else, what drew McCourt to *The Elements of Style* was the person of E. B. White himself. He admired the principled stand White had taken in a public controversy over the practice of magazines accepting corporate sponsorship of articles. McCourt was also impressed by a well-known photograph of White at work in the ten-by-fifteen-foot boathouse where he often wrote. In the photograph, White sits on a bench at a plain wood table, pecking at a manual typewriter, beside a large window opened to the cove that bordered his farm. "E. B. White was at his desk," says McCourt, "and everything was bare, like a Strunk sentence. That was one of the things that drove me to him, too. That kind of honesty and no-nonsense quality."

McCourt eventually found success with *The Elements of Style* in the classroom: "When I moved on to Stuyvesant High School, I taught three junior classes and we got it for them. I had the head of the department order the books. He was kind of a liberal sixties type—not that I wasn't myself—and his eyebrows went up and he wondered why I was using it because, again, the kids were not receptive to rules and regulations. At first, I didn't use it that much because the kids were still resisting it. And there I was struggling with them and I was struggling with Strunk, too—because I'm not capable of getting very far into grammar, style, or anything like that—but there was always E. B. White with this soothing, gentle, humorous voice to carry it along. And I explained to the students that these rules had not emerged full-blown from Strunk's head, that they had come down through the centuries, and that the English language has a history. I remember something that Aristotle said somewhere: that if you understand the history of something, you understand the thing itself. And I tried to explain to them historically how punctuation came about in the English language, and I copied a page of medieval English, where they had practically no punctuation whatsoever, and showed how confused you'd be nowadays if you didn't have punctuation, and how the rules came about—it's all organic, a sentence is an organic thing, and all of that stuff. I think I had some success with that."

The main lesson that McCourt took from *The Elements of Style* and tried to pass along to his students is its insistence on clarity. "Clarity, clarity, clarity—and get rid of adornment and unnecessary words. I went right along with it because I like to get to the point in writing anyway. That's not because I was born with some great gift; it's because of the teaching. Because the kids demand that. The minute you become ambiguous or philosophical, generalized, they're looking at you, and you *know,* because teaching high school kids is such an immediate experience. You can see their eyes drift toward the window if you're not clear and simple. I learned from the classroom experience as much as anything else. And that's why I think I had a particular feeling about Strunk and White—because of their insistence, and because of White's good humor about it more than Strunk. Strunk is funny in his hardheadedness; White is even funnier. It's almost as if they're a vaudeville pair."

Dave Barry: "I came from the English major world, where there wasn't much of an emphasis, that I noticed, on clear and lucid writing, to the journalism world, where at least that's what people said they wanted to do. It was refreshing to know that the book that most people held up as the essential style manual for American English, *The Elements of Style,* advocated that kind of writing. For a while—in my late twenties, early thirties—I was out of journalism and made my living teaching effective writing seminars to businesspeople, and one of the books that I recommended and sometimes read from was *The Elements of Style.* Back then I probably could have quoted a lot of it to you.

It was a good tool for teaching business writing, in the sense that sometimes you just need an authority. What I was trying to teach to my classes was pretty much the Strunk and White ideal, which is to worry about being clear and lucid more than worrying about impressing people. And of course, it requires, I think, a certain level of sophistication with writing to be able to follow that advice. I would use it mostly to stress things like it's better to use the active voice than the passive. Just sort of general things, like omit unnecessary words—the sort of simple, takeaway stuff from the book."

Will Blythe is the author of *To Hate Like This Is to Be Happy Forever,* a personal exploration of the Carolina-Duke basketball rivalry. He is the former fiction editor for *Esquire,* and he contributes to many magazines, including *Harper's, The New Yorker, Rolling Stone, Sports Illustrated,* and *Elle.*

"I can't recall exactly when I first encountered the book—it may have been my last year of high school, in Advanced Placement English, but it could have been later. Until you asked, I probably hadn't looked at it in twenty years, so I reread it. It's one of those books that you think you remember better than you actually do, and it was amazing to see how I reacted to it this time versus how I remembered it.

"I've gone through several stages with Strunk and White. My initial reaction to it—as my reaction back then tended to be when confronted with authority—was to say, 'Oh yeah?' And yet at the same time, I think I bowed to it because I was so intent on learning how to write. But as time went by, I remember coming to feel a great mutiny against the book; I thought it was so Waspy in terms of style that I began to rebel against it. I remember having discussions with people in which I would just absolutely dump all over poor Strunk and White because I thought that it was a repressive book, that it was about a sort of country-club style, where the emphasis was on propriety and so on, that it was a little bow-tie-wearing book. I also saw in it something of the attitude of, say, a gentle but absolutely implacable missionary who believes that he's right and you're probably misguided, but he would never tell you that in a nasty way; he'll do it in such a way that it haunts your conscience.

"But then, as I went back and looked at it for the first time in twenty years, I started thinking this is more like a Taoist manual on how to live, in some ways. I thought that showed up particularly in White's last chapter, 'An Approach to Style,' where he says, 'Place yourself in the background.' I thought, *Yeah, exactly.* Both as a writer and in life, one needn't strain for style, you know? Style is inherent in who one is, so that achieving style is an exercise in becoming more oneself, a methodical stripping away and disclosing of oneself—and I mean that both in life and in writing.

"But the back-and-forth conversation with myself about Strunk and White continued. After having come to this admiration for the Taoist aspect of the book, I thought, *Yes, but there's also still something really Waspy about that notion of style.* It suggests an impatience with neuroses, with vanity, with not knowing who one is, and it has a kind of an innate fear of aggression—all of those are qualities that, in literature, can be not only useful but the very embodiment of one's style. And with many writers, the ideal of simplicity can sometimes be limiting. And so, then, in that sense, Strunk and White began to seem to me not very Jewish, not very Russian, in terms of writers like Dostoyevsky, not very Joycean or word drunk as in the way of *Ulysses,* or even, say, Flann O'Brien and some of those writers. It was hard for me to imagine, for instance, Philip Roth's *Portnoy's Complaint* coming out of a Strunk-and-White state of mind (I hesitate to say 'mind-set,' so recent is my rereading of the great manual that certain words strike me as barbaric).

"Certainly, though, White's essay in Chapter V is the part of the book that I find most simpatico, I think because it seems to come after the fact, after the rules. But that's another interesting point: With any book like this, any so-called manual of rules or principles of style, a question comes up—and I hesitate to use this word because it seems so highfalutin with Strunk and White so recent in my mind—but it raises an *epistemological* question, which is, How can you know these rules unless you already know them? It's like a book on how to sail, for instance; it will mean nothing to you until you've actually gone sailing. To me, Strunk and White makes the most sense after you've spent a lot of time writing and coming, by yourself, through trial and error, to the revelations that are laid down in that book. And then you look at Strunk and White and you think, *That viewpoint, the rules, such as they are, are better absorbed through vast reading and writing; you come to them through induction.* And in that sense, if you come to them early in your career as a writer, as they're laid out here, they may not be all that useful. I don't actually disagree with most of the rules. I think they're good. They make sense to me now, but I don't think they would make as much sense if I hadn't spent a lot of time floundering, which I think is the natural state of writers."

Sharon Olds is one of America's most celebrated poets. *Satan Says,* her first collection of poems, received the San Francisco Poetry Center Award. Her follow-up volume, *The Dead and the Living,* was the 1983 Lamont Poetry Selection and won the National Book Critics Circle Award. Her other books of poems include *The Father; The Wellspring; The Gold Cell; Blood, Tin, Straw; The Unswept Room;* and *Strike Sparks: Selected Poems,*

1980–2002. She has received a National Endowment for the Arts grant and a Guggenheim Foundation fellowship. Her work has appeared in many periodicals and has been widely anthologized. Olds was New York State Poet from 1998 to 2000, and she teaches in New York University's Graduate Creative Writing Program.

"Strunk and White, for me, is more like Strunk and Stuart Little, Strunk and R A D I A N T   P I G [of *Charlotte's Web* fame]. What I remember is a tone of nonchiding common sense and mental health in *The El of Sty*.

"That's how I thought of it, in high school, the *El* referring to the underlying but also uplifted principles of usage, like the elevated railroad (flying subway) of Charlotte's home—grammar being one of the soul's safe houses. And Sty, of course, referred to Wilbur's home, his survival, his nonslaughter. And it didn't hurt that the name *Stuart* came from *Steward*, which came from Sty Warden, guardian of the hogs!

"And *The El of Sty* seemed especially kindly in comparison to a book I loved and hated and read all the time, *The King's English,* by someone with a name like H. M. S. Q. X. Z. Fowler. *King's Eng* was a different kind of book—passionate, sarcastic, obsessed. I did not like what I could sort of smell of its politics, but I adored its examples. Some points of grammar were and are a little beyond my hard wiring: to understand a double negative, I have, to this day, to cover both *not*s with my fingers; my brain on its own can't perform the task of the two canceling each other out.

"So Fowler was out there dancing at the edge of the field of my grammatical I.Q. Sometimes when he'd go beyond my limits, my mind could *stretch* (I could feel it, in my head, *stretching*) and almost get a fine point. It felt as if the gears in my brain disengaged for a moment and I went into a not unpleasurable free fall.

"My thoughts on 'style, clarity, order, and simplicity' in my own work? My poems are like stories; I like for a reader to know who each pronoun stands for, and what's happening. I like to hear a poem by ear before I see it on the page—to experience the music of each different voice and style—and to be using a sense that is much older and more direct than reading by eye. I like in my work for there to be an ordinary chronology—within a poem, and within a book, and in the birth order of the books.

"As for simplicity, there's a bit of a war in me—or more like a birthday-party game, a little savage but not fatal!—I want to be readable to my fellow shoppers at ShopRite (where I buy the wide-ruled school notebooks and the medium black ballpoint pens I write with), but I love weird words, especially their dense physicality. Sometimes one impulse wins out, sometimes the other.

"And sometimes I write first drafts which are like puzzles, or riddles, with a slow reveal, but mostly, in revision, I go back near the beginning and put in a line—or do it with a title—so the reader knows, while reading, pretty much what I know while writing.

"And if anyone knows of any STUART LITTLE or CHARLOTTE'S WEB stickers, I am in the market for them!"

4

The Happiness Boys

In these latter days many bright people who
are supposed to be teaching English composition
have gone whoring after strange gods.

—JACK CASE

I n 1957, *Jack Case* and Harry Cloudman were, respectively, editor and assistant director of Macmillan's College Department. *The Elements of Style* was to be released into both the college and the general (or trade) markets, but it was crucial that the book be well received in English departments around the country. Case, Cloudman, and White were all aware that the 1918 edition was something of a throwback, in terms of then-current academic fashion. On seeing the book in 1957, for the first time in thirty-eight years, White wrote to Howard Stevenson, the friend who had sent it to him: "I take it no use is made of it by the English Department in this day and age; it would be considered too arbitrary, too cocky, too short."

Jack Case confirmed White's suspicions but made the case that English departments around the country stood in need of just the kind of medicine that Strunk was prescribing. In a letter to White in May 1958, Case wrote:

Dear Mr. White:

. . . A final word on prospects for the Little Book: you may not have noticed it, but in these latter days many bright people who are supposed to be teaching English composition have gone whoring after strange gods, and this pursuit seems to have conferred upon them the gift of tongues, though in no two instances the same tongue. They are conducting acrimonious debates with the makers of grammars and dictionaries, living and dead, and with each other, in the presence of the freshman, and God knows what he thinks of it all. The matter of this brawl—such questions as whether there are or ought to be such things as parts of speech, and, if so, what they should be called, may appear of some moment to as many as one hundredth of one per cent of the literate speakers of English, though I doubt it.

Some of us believe that many teachers who have been trying to tell freshmen how to achieve good or at least decent writing are about to get very sick of this noise. We think that, especially where their students are reasonably literate to start with, these teachers would find relief and delight in being able to hand their freshmen a straight-talking little book, with an injunction to keep it at their elbows, read and reread it, and write!

At any rate, that is the wager we are willing to make. We hope you will make it with us.

Sincerely yours,
J. G. Case

After White delivered the completed manuscript, Thanksgiving 1958, Case put it through Macmillan's internal editorial gauntlet and compiled a list of notes about "bugs" and proposed fixes. A Macmillan employee from outside the editorial department, Margaret Nicholson, the company's contract and copyright specialist and author of *A Dictionary of American-English Usage*, had expressed to Case her interest in the project and, after reading the manuscript, made her own list of notes about problems she had found in the text. Case sent these two lists to White in early December 1958. In the meantime, Case had enlisted the help of a consultant, a professor of English, who reviewed both the manuscript and Case's and Nicholson's notes, and submitted a report to Case reflecting both his own opinions and those of some colleagues in academia. In mid-December 1958, Case sent the professor's report to White and introduced, as gingerly as he could, the cautionary note that was being voiced by the consultant.

December 12, 1958

Dear Mr. White:

. . . Bill brought his stuff to the office yesterday and we discussed the project for a while. He is still enthusiastic about it, but he has one great and chilling fear, which we cannot help sharing. It concerns the single-purpose, one-track mind of the descriptive linguist and his less learned next of kin, the anything-goes-in-usage "liberal". For convenience I shall treat these creatures as one. Almost every English department of any size now shelters at least one of these shrill messiahs. They dearly love, and will fight at the drop of a hat for, any non-standard locution adopted by the man in the street, or used once, absentmindedly or for a special purpose, by anyone of note, from Chaucer to Hemingway, and they will tolerate no disapproval of such peccadilloes. One of these aggressive fellows on a textbook committee can put the

other members on the defensive—it's hell to be accused of not being modern. As a result, an excellent book that is not wholly neutral and permissive with regard to usage often is dismissed from consideration after only perfunctory defense by the majority, who would be quite happy with it, but who can't stand being considered old fogies.

I indicated in a letter of last May that, regarding problems of usage, we thought the time might be ripe for a stance that was simple, direct, unpretentious, but with some backbone in it, and we still believe this. Moreover, it is clear to us that anyone who read your preface and the last chapter could not regard this book, or even Strunk's material, as rigidly prescriptive on all levels. The trouble is, as Bill Gibson has pointed out, the people in question don't look at the whole book. They turn at once to the usage section to see how prescriptive you are on like . . . as, shall . . . will, the split infinitive, and a few other points, and reject the text or consider it further, on the basis of that one issue. I'm sure that's hard to believe of people intelligent enough to teach English. It's true.

I am sure that none of us would want to represent Professor Strunk as sanctioning something of which he did not approve and that he would not sanction if he were alive today. However, I think we can and should handle the matter by inserting after this or that prohibition the words "in formal writing", and a statement recognizing that in informal discourse the rule is commonly not observed. I have a feeling that if Professor Strunk were here and knew how the world had moved, he would think it sensible to recognize that what is appropriate on the level of full-dress writing is not obligatory on the level of informal prose or casual talk. Indeed, I imagine he knew all about this, but that he naturally followed the prevailing pattern of concern with the formal level only. A little unbending here would give us some solid ground on which to meet the attacks of the descriptive enthusiasts, and on it, with our other strengths, I think we could repel them as often as not. We do need that much of a chance against particularly fanatical assailants.

The foregoing has to do mainly, in the usage section, with different than, *however,* like-as, shall-will, *and* that-which, *but you might keep an eye open for other spots where a slightly more relaxed attitude would be both justifiable and expedient. The splendid image of Sergeant Strunk, snapping orders and feeling, quite reasonably, no obligation to tell beginners the whole, bloody, complicated truth about anything, is not likely to fade perceptibly as a result of these ministrations, and we shouldn't want it to. . . .*

That's all. I hope it won't blight your Christmas. With best wishes to you and Mrs. White for a merry above,

> *Sincerely,*
> *J. G. Case*

Allowing for the several days it undoubtedly took for Case's letter to find its way from New York City to the farm in North Brooklin, Maine, White's response was immediate. It was also sharp and unequivocal. He was upset.

17 December 1958

Dear Mr. Case:

I have removed "Introductory" and the book now has five chapters, not six. Instead of quoting Strunk's remarks in my "Note", as you suggested, I paraphrased them, which seemed quicker and less fussy.

The Vanity Fair *quote is gone, and I was delighted to see it go. In its place are a few opening sentences from* Northanger

Abbey; *there is nothing loose about them, and they are funny. I like this better than Mr. Gibson's* Howard's End *quote, which, out of context, seemed not to pull together. But before Gibson's notes arrived I had been reading Forster, and I have a quote from* Two Cheers for Democracy *that I like and that you might prefer to the Jane Austen. I will send it along.*

I was busy working a lot of your and Miss N's suggestions into the text, wherever we were in agreement, when your letter came along (December 12th date) and stopped me cold. Do you remember that wonderful moment in the McCarthy hearings when Mr. Welch turned to Mr. Cohn and in his high, friendly voice asked, "And now, Mr. Cohn, when you found that one-third of the photograph was missing, were you saddened?" (Such a wonderful verb for little Mr. Cohn.) Anyway, I was saddened by your letter—the flagging spirit, the moistened finger in the wind, the examination of entrails, and the fear of little men. I don't know whether Macmillan is running scared or not, but I do know that this book is the work of a dead precisionist and a half-dead disciple of his, and that it has got to stay that way. I have been sympathetic all along with your qualms about "The Elements of Style", but I know that I cannot, and will-shall not, attempt to adjust the unadjustable Mr. Strunk to the modern liberal of the English Department, the anything-goes fellow. Your letter expresses contempt for this fellow, but on the other hand you seem to want his vote. I am against him, temperamentally and because I have seen the work of his disciples, and I say the hell with him. If the White-Strunk opus has any virtue, any hope of circulation, it lies in our keeping its edges sharp and clear, not in rounding them off cleverly.

In your letter you are asking me to soften up just a bit, in the hope of picking up some support from the Happiness Boys, or, as you call them, the descriptivists. (I can write you an essay on like-as, *and maybe that is the answer to all this; but softness is not.) I am used to being edited. I like being edited, and I have had the good luck and the pleasure of being edited by some of the best of them; but I have never been edited for wind direction, and will not be now. Either Macmillan takes Strunk and me in our bare skins, or I want out. I feel a terrible responsibility in this project, and it is making me jumpy. And if I have misread or misconstrued your letter, I ask your forgiveness and your indulgence.*

The above, written by the below, are, of course, fighting words, and will, I am sure, bring you out of your corner swinging. But I think it is best that I get them down on paper. I want to get back to work, make progress, and make a good book, and until we get this basic thing straightened out, there isn't much chance. It is ghostly work, at best; and surrounded as I have been lately by a corps of helpers, all of them trying to set me on the right path, it is unnerving work. Your letter did unsettle me on a number of counts.

All this leads inevitably to like-as, different than, *and the others. I will let them lay for the moment, sufficient unto this day being the etc. My single purpose is to be faithful to Strunk as of 1958, reliable, holding the line, and maybe even selling some copies to English Departments that collect oddities and curios. To me no cause is lost, no level the right level, no smooth ride as valuable as a rough ride, no* like *interchangeable with* as, *and no ball game anything but chaotic if it lacks a mound, a box, bases, and foul lines. That's what Strunk was about, that's what I am about, and that (I hope) is what the book is about. Any attempt to tamper with this prickly design will get nobody nowhere fast.*

Another thing that has disturbed me has nothing to do with you or Macmillan—it is that when I reread my piece on style, it left me with a cold feeling of having failed. I am reasonably well satisfied with the gist of it—that is, the advice, the reminders; but

*the introductory section not only failed to invigorate me but left
me wondering whether a lot of it shouldn't just come out of there.
I would welcome your advice. I started the thing quite differently,
in earlier drafts, and arrived much sooner at the main body of the
piece.*

> *Sincerely,*
> *E. B. White*

*P.S. When I said, above, that Macmillan would have to take me in
my bare skin, I really meant my bare* as.

Twenty-four years later, writing to his biographer, Scott Elledge, White recalled this two-page, single-spaced chastisement as a "snotty" letter. He hadn't been sure whether he should mail it to Case, he told Elledge, "it sounded so cocky." But he was glad he had. "It would have been cowardly of me to back down at the last minute after having arranged Will's apotheosis." As it happened, Case and Cloudman were charmed by White's reply. Case wrote back:

> *December 22, 1958*

Dear Mr. White:

*In moments when I have delighted in your scorn of Detroit's
"motivational-research monkeys", Hollywood's pulse-takers, and
the hard-word-easy-word scale of Mr. Rudolf Flesch, I have not
supposed that I could be on the receiving end of this particular
lash. Half an hour ago I opened your letter and Harry Cloudman
and I read it together. We looked up from it with broad grins, in
which, I assure you, there was nothing of the sickly.*

*I said, "All right. He won't go on the defensive. Maybe we
ought to let him take the offensive and whale hell out of 'em."*

Harry said, "I think we should. I'd like to see him do it."

We both knew that "let" was the wrong verb; that you will do what you see clearly you should do, and that your sight is mysteriously clear.

Need I explain our position? Not one time in ten thousand is the textbook writer an artist, writing for an audience of one, which not to do is, as you say with utter, ultimate truth, to be the same as dead, whether a good living be gained or not.

As textbook publishers a large part of our work is the holding of the moistened finger in the wind, the ear to the ground. Do teachers want to begin trigonometry with the general angle or the acute? Do teachers of government want to cover national, state, and local governments in sequence, or do they prefer to treat the executive on all levels, then the legislative on all, and so on? Fortunately, it is not necessary for an editor to take a philosophical position with regard to the acute angle, and I sometimes envy my next door office neighbor, who presides over such placid entities.

Your part of the book, the last chapter and other extended portions, is art; it has its proper criteria, and is not subject to poll-taking. Mr. Strunk's part seems closer to our usual fare—the work of a good man with strong opinions, who in his day probably was correct in thinking, if he did, that most teachers agreed with him and would find his work usable if they wanted a very brief book. He may not have cared a damn whether they agreed with him or not, but they were sure to; there simply was no dissent in these matters. As Bill Gibson has pointed out, this was the pre-levels-of-usage era. Training in English concerned itself with the formal level. . . .

Even if we had no scruples in the matter we should, I hope, be smart enough not to ask you to betray principles to which you adhere and to which you think Mr. Strunk would adhere, if he were teaching in 1958. You can imagine better than we what a 1958-model Strunk would be like; whether his attitude would have

relaxed somewhat, in keeping with the spirit of your chapter—
"There are no taboos." Certainly he would not have become an
"anything goes" radical; he might have become a moderate, with
the great majority of present English teachers.

I mustn't use words like "majority"; they suggest nose-counting
again, adjustment, and the other things that, as an artist, you
rightly condemn. This is as strange a situation for us as it is
for you. In part we are dealing with a work of art (which you
may prefer to call just "writing") which goes straight into the
consciousness of the individual consumer and is self-validating.
And in part we are dealing, as we usually are, with something that
has to pass muster as a usable textbook with not all teachers of
English but with a sizeable block of them.

As far as Harry Cloudman and I are concerned, if we have to
choose, we'll desert the ear-to-the-ground canniness of our often-
dreary profession, and plump for art, knowing nothing stronger in
which to put our faith to carry the day.

So it's all up to you. Just don't, please, in fairness to your old
teacher, let him dwell on things that are of no consequence to
anybody now, or look ridiculous with entries like that on "one-
hundred-and", with the "and" consecrated by all usage from King
Alfred to date.

About the piece on style and your displeasure with the first
part: I have been so close to this now for some time, and have
enjoyed it so much, that I was momentarily surprised at your
reaction. It is better prose than any of us reads in a month of
Sundays, and only by standards as high as yours could it possibly
be thought that you had failed. On second thought I remembered
that when I first read this part, after the New Yorker piece and
the Note, I felt in the first two pages that your casting arm had
stiffened a trifle; then as you got to playing with Paine, Wolfe, and
Frost, it seemed to limber up; the cast came back into rhythm,
and one saw the lovely curves of the line and heard the little, soft

*whishes of the fly before it lighted softly, seemingly without effort,
just where you wanted it.*

*I'm not sure the start should be shorter; perhaps it should be
longer—a somewhat slower cast while you are getting out line. I'm
going up to Toronto for a few days and taking the piece along, but I
doubt that any further reflections of mine on it can help you. You'll
get it the way you want it.*

Again, Merry Christmas.

> *Sincerely,*
> *J. G. Case*

The early dispute concerning the "modern liberal of the English Department" proved a harbinger. This despite the fact that, on publication in the spring of 1959, *The Elements of Style* was almost instantly successful in both the general trade and college markets, to the extent that Macmillan struggled to keep up with reprints and reorders. That summer, colleges began snapping it up for their campus bookstores, and in the fall, adoptions for class use, in both colleges and high schools, were unusually high. But while sales were good, the majority of reviews were positive, and schools embraced the book, it did, as anticipated, take a few early lumps from academic critics of the sort that Jack Case had warned about. A review in the journal *College Composition and Communication* sniffed that the book was "a curious mixture and something less than an adequate textbook for a college course in composition. . . . Both are rules men; neither addresses himself to the positive, the creative aspect of teaching—the nurture of the young mind to the point where it can produce a draft worth revising."

White's decision to retain Strunk's tone and many of his prescriptive admonitions was a sound one and was probably essential to the book's success, but the Strunkian ethos, even if graced by White's ameliorating touches, has been a source of contention into the present. For its size, and for all its popularity in the classroom over the past fifty years, *The Elements of Style* has considerable power to chafe certain strains of academic. "Strunk and White were a pair of hypocritical old grousers whose inaccurate grammar and usage edicts dated not from the last century but the one before that," says the linguist Geoffrey Pullum, not a half-bad old grouser himself. In his academic writings, and online, Pullum has crusaded against "Strunk and White's toxic little compendium of bad grammatical advice" with unflagging vehemence, in the tone of someone who might have been beaten with the book as a child. He is, for instance, irritated that White cautions against the overuse of modifiers *while using them himself. Hypocrisy!* "You don't get good at writing by deleting adjectives," Pullum says, and he notes that most writing contains about 6 percent adjectives, "whether they're good or bad." White, of course, is not concerned with tallying parts of speech. His point, as he makes clear in Chapter V, Rule 4, is that instead of relying on a modifier to prop up a weak noun or verb, writers should work harder to discover and employ stronger, more precise nouns and verbs—the statistical data notwithstanding. The trimming of unnecessary modifiers has been a recognized mark of good style since at least the time of Aristotle, who advised against adding "ornamental epithets to commonplace nouns."

ELMORE LEONARD

The thing is, adverbs can get in the way. And they have nothing to do with the character. If you're writing from the character's point of view, you want to stick with the character and his attitude, his sound. If you've done him right, and if you know who he is, you don't need the adverb.

> In rule 4, in my *10 Rules of Writing*, I say: "Never use an adverb to modify the verb 'said' . . . he admonished gravely. To use an adverb this way (or almost any way) is a mortal sin. The writer is now exposing himself in earnest, using a word that distracts and can interrupt the rhythm of the exchange. I have a character in one of my books tell how she used to write historical romances 'full of rape and adverbs.' "

The English professor Jodi Lundgren, writing in *The Journal of Teaching Writing* in 2000, damns *Elements* on the grounds of gender politics and class-based prejudice. The writer to whom Strunk and White speak, she asserts, is "a white, middle-class, heterosexual male who is here not enjoined to interrogate his privilege but to revel in its self pleasure." Her article "Interrogating the Popularity of Strunk and White" sieves the text for the elements of offense—slighted or undervalued women, militaristic overtones, conventional morality, overt masculinity, even phallic connotations (the word *erect* in White's introduction catches her eye)—and avoids entirely any assessment of the book on its own simple merits as a guide to clear, effective writing.

Another feminist critique, "Bewhiskered Examples in *The Elements of Style*," is offered by Professor Debra Fried, who works on Strunk's home ground in the Cornell English Department. Writing in *Western Humanities Review* in 1991, Fried looks closely at usage examples in *The Elements of Style* and finds that the two men have written a book with an irritatingly male point of view. Among the troubling evidence she finds in Strunk and White's "pernicious" examples are a woman with many children and an ironing board ("a dreary picture of female domestic slavery," says Fried), another who "smells good, as a pretty girl should," and yet another who is portrayed as indecisive. Along the way, she hatches a weirdly riveting argument for the colon as a mark of punctuation with patriarchal overtones.

The irony, missed by even the book's strongest critics (and the stronger the critique, the more pronounced the irony), is that in their own writing, particularly in those portions of it that work best, those same critics faithfully observe the main tenets of the Strunk and White doctrine even while cursing it.

A reader sent White a review of *The Elements of Style* that misquoted Strunk as having advised writers to "Use Less Words!"

Dear Mr. _____

I often wish Strunk could come alive, so that I might hear the gnashing of his teeth. He would have loved "Use less words." I love it, too. But I would like to watch him leaping at some of our non-words, like "input." I would like to hear him on the subject of "a viable alternative." I would like to hear what he says about "simplistic." Or even "a multidisciplinary approach to quality care," may God forgive me.

Thanks for your letter and the review.

Sincerely,
E. B. White

Professor Keith Hjortshoj is the director of the Writing in the Majors program in Cornell University's Knight Institute for Writing in the Disciplines, an interdisciplinary complex of writing programs unaffiliated with the English Department. Hjortshoj says that while *The Elements of Style* remains popular at Cornell and elsewhere, he has his doubts about its utility. "The appeal of Strunk and White's book lies in the attractiveness of the myth that it creates," he says. "It's a wonderful myth that applies not just to writing, but to all kinds of endeavors: that there's a simple way to do this, and that amazingly talented, brilliant practitioners demonstrate that you can reduce it to a little compendium of rules or procedures. White was the ideal person to either create or perpetuate that myth with writing because he was such an amazing prose stylist. He had mastered the ability to turn phrases without any apparent effort; writing that he had put enormous amounts of effort into seemed utterly effortless and casual, as though anyone could do it. And everybody did want to do it—his reputation as an essayist was just so huge and well deserved."

In *Teaching Prose: A Guide for Writing Instructors,* Hjortshoj further describes the "myth" of *The Elements of Style,* and its effects on students and instructors alike:

> *The Elements of Style* is especially popular at Cornell, its birthplace, where stacks of these tiny volumes sell like hotcakes in the campus store, and where faculty and students often announce in a glow of virtue that they have read it cover-to-cover and that it did them a world of good, as though it were the New Testament. My own view is that *The Elements of Style* demonstrates E. B. White's remarkable skill at drawing the reader into compelling little myths about ordinary things. The myth in this case is that White, with the ghostly voice of William Strunk still ringing in his ears, miraculously condensed everything everyone needs to know about writing into 85 pages, available for the price of a plain pizza. We all wish it were true.

Mythical or not, in a recent spring semester at Cornell, *The Elements of Style* was an assigned text in no fewer than twenty classes (only two of those in the English Department). Cornell professors who have assigned *The Elements of Style,* in areas ranging from art history to industrial and labor relations, from psychology to marine sciences, say it addresses many of the problems they see in student papers, and it gives positive results. "The book offers a terrific, concise set of instructions and commentary on basic word usage and sentence construction," says Professor Lowell Turner, Chair of International and Comparative Labor in the School of Industrial and Labor Relations. "So many of the mistakes my students make (and these are Cornell upper-division undergraduate students) are addressed in Strunk and White." Professor Isabel Hull, an author and an instructor in Cornell's History Department, says she assigns *The Elements of Style* "because it remains the best single, shortest, pithiest text on the subject. Students can read it quickly and absorb it straightaway." As for results, Hull says it works: "I receive comments from past students (the last one was ten days ago from a student from 1982), all of whom without exception praise the improvement in their writing, and consequently in their thinking, from following these principles in my classes." A graduate student and teacher in the Knight Institute Taryn Chubb says, "I think it works well for students who really want to improve their writing and are willing to take the time to apply what Strunk and White say. I always get results when I have students read the sections on inflated language and needless words."

Professor Hjortshoj himself allows that the book may have some useful virtues for students who are interested in improving their writing. "It's so little it certainly can't hurt them to read it," he says. "I think there might be glimmers—that if they actually looked a little bit at their own work and thought about those rules—that they could gain something from it. I think professional writers can as well. Academic writers certainly can because the emphasis it places on simplicity and concision is a message that writers in academics have to remember all the time. Everything that happens linguistically in a place like this gets more and more complicated and more and more compressed and congested. I see it all the time in scientific writing, for example. That piece I wrote [from *Teaching Prose*] sounds scathing. But I didn't quite mean it that way. It's a lovely little myth to remember and sort of keep with you, to sort of keep your bearings, I guess. If I'm skeptical about the book, it's because of the ways it's used—by teachers who think they can just assign this book to students and it will refine their prose—not because of its origins. It's not that I think White was being dishonest. I think he was being pretty clever. And in fact, his chapter on style at the end of the book is quite honest about the complexity of this problem."

NICHOLSON BAKER

You can think of *The Elements of Style* as a kind of hose. The thing that you're trying to say is rough, it's muddy, it's all broken and caulked-together and it's got handprints on it—and you play the hose of clarity over it so as to see its structure better and melt away some of the excrescences. You don't want to melt everything away because then you end up with some terrible cast-iron substructure. You just want to see the form of the thought a little better—and there's where Strunk and White comes in handy sometimes. The book is a useful hose.

The teaching of writing in American schools and universities has been as philosophically wobbly and fad-prone as the weight-loss industry. Trends in writing instruction have ebbed and flowed in response to social movements, population shifts, varying birthrates, expanding access to education, and changes in the hoped-for results of student writing programs (plotted on a continuum running from the utilitarian to the artistic—i.e., from employment to self-expression). Approaches to teaching writing have come at the problem from most imaginable angles—by first grounding young writers in Latin and Greek; by emphasizing the study of literature; by applying derivatives of Aristotle's rhetorical principles; and often by pushing aside Latin, Greek, literature, and Aristotle and trying other things.

If the English departments of 1958 were whoring after strange gods, the decades that followed found the same departments undergoing a transformation that neither E. B. White nor Jack Case could have imagined. Will Strunk would likely be glad he missed it. Through the 1960s and 1970s, mirroring the social and cultural transformations of the Beatles–to–Blitzkrieg Bop era, the educational terrain was shifting in ways both obvious and subtle, profoundly affecting English departments and the humanities generally. As writing programs experimented with freewriting, self-expression, and other zeitgeist-fueled approaches, the literary studies side of the department was enduring the manifold infiltrations of postmodernism and the spreading morass of "theory" inspired by the writings of thinkers such as Jacques Derrida, Michel Foucault, and Jacques Lacan. Today's composition programs are the heirs to and practitioners of a mind-bending variety of pedagogical philosophies, many drawing on classic rhetorical models, but "complicated" (to use the preferred bit of jargon) by the thousand and one hot-button sensitivities young scholars are asked to "interrogate" (another bit) within the realms of class, culture, gender, race, history, politics, power, authority, economics, ecology, technology, colonialism, and, surely by now, climatology.

"English departments and their values came under severe and mean attack over the last thirty years," says Dr. Michael Carson, professor of English at the University of Evansville. "A host of ideologies attacked the dead white guys and called into question not only what was being taught and what needed to be taught, the subject matter, but also how it was being taught. You can graduate from good undergraduate schools now with an English major and not have studied Shakespeare. In Huxley's *Brave New World,* the government takes away Shakespeare and locks it up, and, ironically, thanks to the political infighting in the schools today, many English departments have really taken great literature away from the students; it's just horrifying. This has important consequences because at every level—politically, morally, and artistically—those who are not literate are not equipped to remain free. Democracy can only exist when people can use their own language and negotiate their way through ideas and problems. You can't have society without rationality. And rationality demands clarity. I am unwilling to dignify the jargon term *postmodern* with discussion time in class. If one of my students uses that word categorically as if it is a given, I'll say, 'What do you mean? What are you talking about? Go back and think.' "

DAVE BARRY

It's amazing how much studying you can do about writing and talking about writing and listening to people talk about writing without hearing any really clear, simple advice. *The Elements of Style* is so direct and positive and specific. I don't want to tar the entire academic profession, but there doesn't seem to be a lot of that kind of writing going on in the world of academe. I don't get the impression that being clear and simple and lucid is a goal of most academic writers, so I don't know when kids would get exposed to it. Many people who buy *Elements*, I'm guessing, are, for the most part, people like my former students, who kind of got thrown out into the world and suddenly had to write not for papers and not for grades, but just so people would know what the hell they were talking about. There's amazingly little advice about how to do that. We sort of go from teaching our kids to spell and some fundamental rules of grammar to having them write essays and encouraging them to write whatever they want. It's gotten even worse now with the Internet and blogs, where anybody can write anything. It's good in the sense that people are writing a lot—I'm always sort of relieved that the Internet is such a text-oriented medium—but there clearly isn't that much guidance about how to do it well.

One of the lasting legacies of the whirlwind of "theory" (described by one critic as "inept philosophy applied to literature and culture") that has swept through the educational establishment is a deep suspicion of claims of knowledge and a distrust in the existence of truth and any of its associated implications about our moral nature. Claims about meaning and truth, theory tells us, are fictions or, at best, locally contingent beliefs created within specific contexts of gender, race, cultural and economic status, et cetera. Since the varieties of context and contingency are endless, the idea that objective truth can be arrived at, much less accurately described and communicated by a writer to a reader, is an illusion, and truth itself a mirage as unachievable as the horizon. Whatever else a theory-based education imparts, it seems most effective at leaving students with the firm conviction that they'll never have another firm conviction, that they will never again be able to utter one unequivocally true statement—an unnerving prospect for anyone, much more so for the aspiring writer.

Given the current political and ideological bent of the humanities, is it any wonder that *The Elements of Style,* while thriving in the sciences and elsewhere across the curriculum, is sometimes unwelcome in the modern English department? Thrumming away inside this book about style is a most unstylish idea, but an idea that is also one of the most durable, encouraging, and commonsensical notions ever to inspire a student or fire the mind of a writer: the belief that careful, clear thinking and writing can uncover truth.

To believe in Strunk and White is to believe that truth exists and that commitment to clarity is the path to it. Think of it as an axiom of natural law for writers—the deep, abiding, and enabling fact that allows all writers, even the theorists, to get their work done. It's not the arrogance of claiming that you have got your arms around the *totality* of truth, that you have found *the answer;* it's rather the simple confidence that, through clear observation and thinking, you can at least touch some aspects of truth and, with a little diligence and care, bring facets of reality home intact for your readers. Dr. Robert Kane, professor of philosophy at the University of Texas and author of *Through the Moral Maze,* puts it this way: "Postmodernists believe that we can't be certain of the objective truth because we can't get the whole of it. And therefore, they infer that it doesn't exist. But I'm suggesting to you that this is a mistake. All that follows is that we can never be sure we have the *whole* truth, not that there is no truth to be found."

At age twenty-nine, two years after going to work full-time for Harold Ross, E. B. White wrote to his older brother Stanley about the pleasures of the kind of writing he was getting to do at *The New Yorker:* "Sometimes in writing of myself—which is the only subject anyone knows intimately—I have occasionally had the exquisite thrill of putting my finger on a little capsule of truth, and heard it give the faint squeak of mortality under my pressure, an antic sound." Years later, in the fifth chapter of *The Elements of Style,* he would state this article of faith with force: "If one is to write one must believe—in the truth and worth of the scrawl, in the ability of the reader to receive and decode the message."

ALEC WILKINSON

In a way, when I read disordered prose I think, *Okay, this is written by somebody whom I can't trust.* Because the writer isn't willing to do the work to make clear what he or she wants to say and to say it well. It seems to be enough—in this age of Internet rants and talk radio and things like that—to be passionate or to have a point of view to defend. It doesn't seem so important to strive to do it articulately or elegantly. And for me, the whole idea is that clarity is elegant. I think of the phrase of William Maxwell's, used as the title of his collected correspondence with Frank O'Connor, it's "the happiness of getting it down right." It's the job done well. And if people want to level criticism at *The Elements of Style* from the point of view that it's too didactic or moralizing, I suppose they could justify it. But I'd like to say: Really? Show me something better. Show me a better model. *Lack* of clarity? Slovenliness? Sloppiness? Show me something better.

Questions of objective truth often come interlaced with questions of morality, another subject that makes the professoriat nervous. If certainty is bad, *moral* certainty is the worst kind of bad. In more than one academic critique over the years, *The Elements of Style* has been scrutinized for signs of didacticism and moral chauvinism. The professor of philosophy Berel Lang, in a 1982 article titled "Strunk and White and Grammar as Morality," writes that Strunk and White present readers with a modern moral allegory. "In it," Lang writes, "we see the outline of a continuing moral struggle between the forces of good and the forces of evil, a struggle by Strunk and White on the side of the Good (under the guise of grammatical instruction) in a Manichean world where pretension, pomposity, carelessness, and opacity pit their easy charms against the unadorned and severe demands of simplicity, directness, and sincerity." He may have overstated the case slightly—*The Elements of Style* as *Star Wars* sequel—but I don't believe either Strunk or White would strongly object to Lang's interpretation.

A reader chided White for using the phrase *parvum opus* in the introduction to *The Elements of Style* then telling writers, in Chapter V, to avoid foreign languages. "Do you write the rules and not obey them?"

Dear Mr. _____

"Parvum opus" means "small work," as distinct from the familiar "magnum opus", which means important or large work. I break my own rules when I use a word or phrase from another language. Latin, however, isn't a "foreign"

*language, it's a dead language. To me it's very much alive—
at the root of many of our words.*

Sincerely,
E. B. White

It is worth noting that, whatever it consists of, the moral component of *The Elements of Style* is not a question of *religious* proselytizing, for despite the fact that Moses and Jesus both show up on page 1, in Rule 1, thus securing the book's bona fides as an artifact of Judeo-Christian culture, neither author was particularly religious in the conventional sense. But the moral thread running through *The Elements of Style* is undeniable. The only question seems to be whether it belongs there. The argument is between those who find moral overtones of any shade, no matter how muted, distressing if not repugnant, as if a book should or could be created in a moral vacuum, and those to whom a moral viewpoint is seen as a natural attribute of any artist's creation. "Clear writing and goodness are related; they go together," says Dr. Carson. "The people who say there is a disjunction between clarity of mind or soul and clarity of language are the ones who have to prove that. History and everyday experience are on the side of those who say that clarity of mind, clarity of soul, and clarity of language are one thing. As Ben Jonson said, 'Language most shows a man: Speak, that I may see thee.' You are what you say."

E. B. White himself did not shy from bringing morality into the discussion of style. "Muddiness is not merely a disturber of prose," he wrote, "it is also a destroyer of life, of hope." Near the end of "An Approach to Style," as he draws together the threads of his doctrine, White says, "As an elderly practitioner once re-marked, 'Writing is an act of faith, not a trick of grammar.' This moral observation would have no place in a rule book were it not that style *is* the writer, and therefore what a man is, rather than what he knows, will at last determine his style."

TRUTH

Another theme undergirding *The Elements of Style* is the belief that by working to achieve clarity in one's thinking, observing, and writing, one has a real hope of arriving at some truth about the world and communicating it successfully to readers. This simple and, to some, obvious fact has been challenged by the deflating and dispiriting impact of "theory" and all its related isms in the modern classroom. In my conversations with writers, we touched on the real or imagined impact of theory, postmodernism, and the like, and on the search for truth in their own work.

Will Blythe: "Well, [from the postmodern point of view] there's no truth to point to unless it's *their* particular truth, which is that there's no truth to point to, right? I always have that problem with the claim that all truths are relative. The idea that all truths are relative is put forward as a truth in and of itself, so philosophically, it's always seemed to me to be a weak position. But I really come down somewhere in the middle, because the making of good sentences, how you arrive at them, is such a mysterious act in some ways. From both philosophical approaches, you may end up with sentences that have something in common, which is a kind of transparency, a kind of clarity. And I don't mean they're necessarily simple.

"Think of a writer like William Gass, with his sometimes very self-conscious rhetoric. Even William Gass's sentences, when he's at his most highly rhetorical, still have a great deal of clarity as individual sentences, if you can figure out what they mean. Of course, clarity has come under assault as a more malleable value than we originally thought. *The Elements of Style* was probably a great target when the Derrida enthusiasts took over university English departments. It was probably a perfect kind of book for them to perform their operations on, because it purports to have these sort of ideologically neutral biases. Clarity, I think, was probably one of those ostensibly transparent values or ideologically neutral values that somebody reading from the perspective of, say, Jacques Derrida performing a deconstructionist act, would have thought, No, it's not, actually. It depends on *whose* clarity, you know?"

Nicholson Baker: "If people have something interesting to say, it's interesting because they're trying to say something true. It can be playful and it can be funny, but the urge to tell the truth is basic to all these different things—to writing essays, to doing muckraking journalism, to writing complicated novels in which people just sit and talk, all those kinds of things. You have something that you've noticed, something that you want to get down; you desperately want to tell people the truth.

"I have lost touch with things like postmodernism. I don't even think the word means anything at this point. But take a word like *issues,* for instance, the word *issues* being used in place of *problems*—that's a failure of clarity. I mean, if a thing is a problem, it's a problem. It isn't an issue. On the other hand, you have to say, to be truthful, that the urge to say things gently and not to hurt people's feelings is kind of a lovable quality, so somebody somewhere along the line thought, Well, I don't want to say that this thing I'm talking about is a *problem* because that will hurt the person's feelings, so I'll call it an *issue.* And then it just gets turned into some kind of massive mistake in which everybody repeats this thing, and suddenly the word *issue* is eroded and almost destroyed because it now means 'problem.' This kind of euphemistic creep goes on over and over again. And yet it's part of a kind of appealing human urge not to say things with devastating clarity, but just to say things with a slight slant-edness so that feelings aren't hurt or scandals aren't propagated, that sort of thing."

Ian Frazier: "To me the idea that you can't arrive at truth is a depressing idea. But I never felt that there was such a huge con-tradiction between very clear and objective journalism and really unobjective and unclear journalism. For example, I loved A. J. Liebling and Joseph Mitchell and E. B. White—people who were writing plainly and carefully and with that faith that they were looking to find something true. On the other hand, when I was a kid, I just loved Hunter Thompson. Here was a guy writing from drug stupors sometimes. He was an unreliable journalist in the sense that you had to think, *Well, he sees it this way, but he's just done five hundred hits of mescaline.*

"I think that you can tell the honesty of the writer regardless of the way the person's writing. You can tell that Hunter Thompson was, in those early pieces, a fundamentally honest person. I think it was just real. He was really telling you something. And I think that is as valuable in its way as the simplest and most straightforward and most unpretentious kind of journalism. Over time, as you see in the career of Hunter Thompson, that agonistic method does not hold up because your soul and your physical self cannot sustain it. So I think in terms of economy, the people who keep going and the people who write well conform to the simpler and more sort of faithful, straightforward model of going about finding the truth. A maxim I've always liked is something William Maxwell once said: 'As I get older I put more faith in what actually happened. It has a great meaning if you can only get at it.'"

Alec Wilkinson: "I agree with both sides. Both sides are true. It's just that, even if you take the postmodern point of view and the text really only represents the interior life of the writer, then it is still objectively true about that writer, about that attempt to find clarity. I think the postmodern thing is a reaction to a kind of authorial presumption of privilege and oversight that was not earned. Think of a writer like Norman Mailer, or someone like that; he's an advertisement for the fact that *what I'm saying is clearly only representative of what I believe and have observed.* He's far too self-engaged to be reliable as a witness of any kind. And so you get too many people doing that kind of thing and it creeps into television commentators and radio talk-show hosts and things like that, and at some point the mind rebels and says, *Enough! You're only talking about yourself! What matters to you does not matter to me.* So it's not surprising that that line of thought would emerge in this period of time when the culture, for better or worse, no longer has a unified order to it.

"But I believe they're both true. Somewhere in *My Mentor,* I report about William Maxwell saying to me in a taxi, 'Every time I write something I ask myself, "Is this true?"' I think that advice is as good as any I've heard. And at some point, on anything I write—and I hope this doesn't sound pretentious—but at some point I go through it and say, Is this true? Is this true? And then it's true for me. And it fits both the postmodern idea of Yup, it's true for me, might not be true for you, and it is true in the old sense as well. Think of it as like a cubist portrait, in which my approach to this material is a facet, a plane, a perspective of this portrait, which is done in a cubist style as opposed to the representational figurative style, because the cubist style seems more to answer the way this subject, this material is absorbed by the world. So I think both are right. I don't think it's fashionable these days, probably, to aspire toward truthfulness. I think already any intention to do that is to invalid oneself out of the mainstream, pretty much, but I believe in it. I support it. I endorse it.

"It's an interesting observation postmodernists make, but is it profound? Not really. It's pretty obvious to anybody. There's nothing ground-shaking about it. It changes nothing about the discussion. It merely observes, really, that the discussion has changed, and here's how and why. But what can I do about it, or what can any writer or artist do about it? Pretend to be something or someone one isn't? It's just an opinion. I believe in and I endorse the opinion that White expresses and Strunk expressed because I have found it helpful as a matter of technique to try to convey things in the manner that they recommend: succinctly, intelligently, carefully, with maximum attention."

5

The Fewest Obstacles

The approach to style is by way of plainness,
simplicity, orderliness, sincerity.

—E. B. WHITE

In 1938, E. B. White gave up his weekly job of writing "Notes and Comment" for *The New Yorker*, accepted an offer to write a monthly column for *Harper's* (the essays that were later collected in his celebrated *One Man's Meat*), and moved with his family full-time to their saltwater farm in Brooklin, Maine. Katharine continued working, via mail, editing fiction and poetry for *The New Yorker*, while Andy concentrated on the new column and on the chores around the farm. The Whites had purchased the property in 1933 as a retreat from the stifle and frenzy of New York City, as a place where White could connect with the natural world he had loved since childhood, where Katharine could indulge her passion for gardening, and where the daily labors of small-scale farming could anchor White and provide a pragmatic, real-world counterpoint to the writer's life of the mind. The Whites lived at the farm year-round until 1943, when they returned to New York City to help Harold Ross through a troublesome stretch of diminished manpower at *The New Yorker* during the war. As it turned out, they did not return to full-time residence at the farm until 1957, the year White began work on *The Elements of Style.*

Part of what White was fleeing, or at least gladly putting behind him, by leaving New York City for the seclusion of coastal Maine was a kind of psychic suffocation created by the increasing complexity of big-city life and the attendant expectation, perhaps felt most acutely by a sensitive artist working on one of the leading fronts of culture, that success would, sooner or later, begin to take its interest out in a man's principles. E. B. White had never been much for compromise, and he was suspicious of the agreement he seemed to have struck with the city and its breathless, headlong rush of technology, media, advertising, and consumerism. White wrote about his reasons for leaving New York in an early *Harper's* column:

> What was it? What did it? What finally was too much to bear? It would be hard for me to put my finger on any one thing; rather it was an accumulation of things and the total effect inimical to health and happiness. . . . A certain easy virtue in everyone, myself included, and the willingness to accept the manner and speech of the promoter and the gossip writer. A certain timbre of journalism and the stepping up of news, with the implication that the first duty of man is to discover everything that has just happened everywhere in the world. . . . The acceptance, by individual and state, of the ideal of publicity, as though the sheer condition of being noticed were the ultimate good. . . . These things combined to create something from which I shrank and do shrink, in a city which I loved and do love. It is a little hard to get on paper, but I smell something that doesn't smell good. There is a decivilizing bug somewhere at work.

The move to Maine was White's vote for civility, for a life whose pace felt right to him and whose more elemental challenges he gladly embraced over the galloping hype and not-so-quiet desperation of the city. It was also a move toward a simpler life, though, notably, not a less busy one. In a column titled "Report," written in late 1939, White cataloged the agricultural goings-on at the farm: In his charge were fifteen sheep, 148 laying hens, three geese, six roosters, a pig, a cat, and a dog. He grew hay, oats, apples, pumpkins, squash, potatoes, and beets. The Whites sold eggs (some three hundred dozen that year), canned preserves and jams, and caught copious quantities of cod, haddock, and mackerel. For all the joy he took from his work on the land, and its considerable productivity, White made no claim to be anything other than a writer playing at being a farmer, the proprietor of a "private zoo." "I am farming," he wrote, "to a small degree and for my own amusement, but it is a cheap imitation of the real thing."

In Maine, E. B. White's usual working space was his study in

E. B. White, North Brooklin, Maine
Used by permission of Allene White and the estate of E. B. White.

the front of the farmhouse, across the hall from where Katharine worked on *New Yorker* manuscripts and galleys in her own study. But when the weather was favorable, on mild spring and fall mornings, much of White's writing was launched from a simple 10-by-15-foot boathouse near the water's edge. In the boathouse, he sat on a wooden bench, his typewriter resting atop a simple pine table. A small barrel, a nail keg, was within easy reach, to catch those attempts—yanked from the typewriter carriage with a knurled *zip*, crumpled, and tossed—that failed to

IAN FRAZIER

One of the things I admire about E. B. White is his getting out of the New York fabulous, hip, Algonquin Round Table world and going to Maine. I thought that was a very sound decision. And if you read Dorothy Parker or any of the Round Table people now (a good example being Alexander Woollcott, who's just a windbag bore and nothing of his survives, or somebody like George S. Kaufman even), their witticisms get old, they're stale. Obviously, they had a huge effect in American culture, from movies to early TV and, of course, to writing as well. But to me the real solid work was being done by E. B. White off in Maine. I thought he did better there than the whole bunch of them put together at the Round Table. Just read the beginning of *Charlotte's Web*. It's such an elegantly written book, and it never at any point shows off, it doesn't ever preen. With White you get an actual voice; it's not a voice that he came up with in order to sound different in a conversation at the Algonquin—it's an actual voice.

hit the mark. A large, single-paned awning window at one end of the shed framed a view of Allen Cove, a mile-wide inlet at the southern end of Blue Hill Bay, in the middle of Maine's Atlantic coastline.

White's simple boathouse shared similarities, in both its physical and its metaphysical dimensions, with a more famous structure, the cabin built at Walden Pond by the one literary figure whom White, not known for his enthusiasms in that direction, admired most: Henry David Thoreau. In the opening chapter of *Walden,* the chronicle of his two-year experiment in self-sufficiency on the shore of the pond in Concord, Massachusetts, Thoreau describes the one-room home he built for himself at a cost of twenty-eight dollars, twelve and a half cents:

> I have thus a tight shingled and plastered house, ten feet wide by fifteen long, and eight-feet posts, with a garret and a closet, a large window on each side, two trap-doors, one door at the end, and a brick fireplace opposite.

Thoreau had gone to the woods "to transact some private business with the fewest obstacles." "I wished to live deliberately," he wrote, "to front only the essential facts of life, and see if I could not learn what it had to teach, and not, when I came to die, discover that I had not lived." He seemed to feel something much like the "decivilizing bug" that had pushed White out of the city and into a life more closely tied to the land and to the rhythm of the seasons. And he was an evangelist on the theme of simplicity:

> Our life is frittered away by detail. . . . Simplicity, simplicity, simplicity! I say, let your affairs be as two or three, and not a hundred or a thousand; instead of a million count half a dozen,

and keep your accounts on your thumb-nail. . . . Simplify,
simplify. Instead of three meals a day, if it be necessary eat but
one; instead of a hundred dishes, five; and reduce other things
in proportion. . . . Men think that it is essential that the *Nation*
have commerce, and export ice, and talk through a telegraph,
and ride thirty miles an hour. . . . Why should we live with such
hurry and waste of life?

E. B. White's biographer, Scott Elledge, notes that White was first
smitten with *Walden* at Cornell and that "after he graduated,
when he was trying to avoid a life of what Thoreau called 'self-
imposed bondage,' he was sustained by the example as well as
the doctrine of Thoreau." In 1954, White was asked by *The Yale
Review* to contribute a piece on the hundred-year anniversary of
the publication of *Walden.* In the essay, a forceful consideration
of Thoreau's character and accomplishment, White acknowl-
edged a debt of spirit to Thoreau and praised the "steadiness"
lying at the heart of *Walden,* a quality he described as "confidence, faith, the discipline of looking always at what is to be
seen, undeviating gratitude for the life-everlasting that he found
growing in his front yard." The essay also made explicit the kin-
ship with Thoreau that his spare creative space kindled in White:

Here in the boathouse I am a wilder and, it would appear, a
healthier man, by a safe margin. I have a chair, a bench, a table,
and I can walk into the water if I tire of the land. . . . A mouse
and a squirrel share the house with me. The building is, in fact, a
multiple dwelling, a semidetached affair. It is because I am semidetached while here that I find it possible to transact this private
business with the fewest obstacles. . . . Here in this compact
house . . . I can feel the companionship of the occupant of the
pond-side cabin in Walden woods.

Dear Mrs. _____

Sociologists often appear to be dedicated to the task of making complex what is simple and making abstruse what is obvious. So I doubt that you will be able to get far in your attempt to clean up the language of the sociologists, laudable though the effort may be.

There are very few thoughts or concepts that can't be put into plain English, provided anyone truly wants to do it. But for everyone who strives for clarity and simplicity, there are three who for one reason or another prefer to draw the clouds across the sky.

Sincerely,
E. B. White

Thoreau's plea for simplicity resonated throughout White's life and work. "In our culture of gadgetry and the multiplicity of convenience," he wrote in the *Yale Review* essay, "his cry 'Simplicity, simplicity, simplicity!' has the insistence of a fire alarm." Simplicity, for both Thoreau and White, was not primarily a worry about possessions. It was, rather, a call toward plainness of intention and the challenge of crafting an authentic life, a life as true and lean and fit for its purpose as a Strunk sentence, like a drawing with no unnecessary lines. For both men, that was the life of the writer with close ties to his natural surroundings, the life of thoughtful observation and the careful chronicling of experience, with as much simplicity of craft and of intent as possible. And both men believed that good writing, like a life well lived, hewed to the ideal of simplicity. "As for style of writing," Thoreau wrote, "if one has anything to say, it drops from him simply and directly, as a stone falls to the ground." For Thoreau, writing here at age eighteen, it was the path to perfection on the page:

> If we would aim at perfection in anything, Simplicity must not be overlooked. If the author would acquire literary fame, let him be careful to suggest such thoughts as are simple and obvious, and to express his meaning distinctly and in good language. To do this, he must, in the first place, omit all superfluous orna-mentation, which, though very proper in its place,—if, indeed, it can be said to have any in good composition,—tends rather to distract the mind, than to render a passage more clear and strik-ing, or an idea more distinct. . . . The most sublime and noblest precepts may be conveyed in a plain and simple strain.

White echoed the idea years later, in a 1940 *Harper's* column: "There isn't any thought or idea that can't be expressed in a fairly simple declarative sentence, or in a series of fairly simple declara-tive sentences." For White, the call was not only to the altar of a spare prose style but also to the plain frankness of making his living as a writer. His work and the life made possible by the work were of a piece. "To write a piece and sell it to a magazine," White wrote to his brother Stanley shortly after joining *The New Yorker,* "is as near a simple life as shining up a pushcart full of apples and vending them to passersby. It has a pleasing directness not found in the world of commerce and business."

The quest for simplicity in writing is a reflection of the long-ing for it in one's life as well. Undue, mushrooming complexity is not only the foe of good writing but also the defining quality of modernity, and anyone wishing to approach work, art, or life at a gentler, more human pace must work hard to avoid its effects.

JONATHAN YARDLEY

In a 2008 column paying tribute to *The Elements of Style*, Jonathan Yardley, book critic for *The Washington Post*, noted that *Elements* has been his "constant companion" for fifty years. He uses a first-edition hardcover and mentions in passing that he wouldn't mind if someone tossed it into his casket when the time comes. Yardley writes, "The language takes a daily beating, often from people who, as both Strunk and White point out, are more interested in appearing elegant and erudite than in actually being so, people who believe that pompous, inaccurate language is evidence of deep thought and noble purpose. The truth is the opposite. As White writes: 'Avoid the elaborate, the pretentious, the coy, and the cute. Do not be tempted by a twenty-dollar word when there is a ten-center handy, ready and able.' As both Strunk and White were aware, this is hard advice to follow, for it is much more difficult to be concise than to be verbose. Consider, if you will, the Gettysburg Address on the one hand and the rhetoric of William Jefferson Clinton (or, to be bipartisan, George W. Bush) on the other. It is the difference between eloquence and bloviation, but as Warren Gamaliel Harding well knew, bloviation is a presidential prerogative."

White was feeling those effects in the 1930s. They were nagging at Thoreau as early as 1845, when he wrote that "men have become the tools of their tools." This at a time when the cutting-edge technological breakthroughs were the sewing machine and the stapler, a hundred orders of magnitude removed from today's electronic tethers—laptop, cell phone, BlackBerry. Would anyone be much surprised to learn that Walden Woods now sports Wi-Fi and CCTV security? If Thoreau were to undertake his experiment today, it might be webcast, like a David Blaine stunt, or picked up as a reality show. ("CBS. 8:00–9:00. *Cabin Fever.* Repeat. Henry eats a woodchuck.") In the early *Harper's* essay about his reasons for leaving New York, E. B. White had warned that moderns, "by not resenting and resisting the small indignities of the times, are preparing themselves for the eventual acceptance of what they themselves know they don't want." Such as, perhaps, a life of facile, fidgety entertainment, constant "connectivity," and ever-diminishing expectations of occasional solitude or even simple privacy. The tools of our tools.

Simplicity as a pillar of *The Elements of Style*—plainness as a virtue—comes to the book through both sides of its lineage. In his original introduction, Strunk wrote that the book "aims to give in brief space the principal requirements of plain English style," and he advised young writers to first learn to write "plain English adequate for everyday uses" before turning "for the secrets of style, to the study of the masters of literature." And what is Strunk's scriptural nugget—*omit needless words*—but a crisp reminder to keep things simple? Among E. B. White's confirming contributions in 1959 was the idea that plainness itself could constitute one of the most important "secrets of style." As he put it in Chapter V, "The approach to style is by way of plainness, simplicity, orderliness, sincerity."

ADAM GOPNIK

I have a twelve-year-old son who's learning to write essays and term papers. And the good teachers that he has teach him the right things. They teach him to put his thoughts in consecutive order. They teach him to decide what he's going to say and then go ahead and say it. They teach him to construct a piece logically, where the thesis is at the beginning, the evidence is in the middle, and the conclusion is at the end. And I teach him to always search for the simpler word—whenever you use a complicated word, see if there's a simpler word you can use.

Simplicity as a virtue in writing reaches back to Aristotle and beyond. It's such a self-evident first principle that it may seem too obvious to mention. But it is an expectation so frequently confounded that writers and writing teachers have never tired of pointing it out to would-be practitioners. In the opening paragraphs of *The King's English,* published in 1906 by H. W. and F. G. Fowler (Harold Ross's favorite grammarian, Henry Fowler, writing with his brother, Francis), writers are advised to be direct, simple, brief, vigorous, and lucid. The Fowlers illustrate:

This general principle may be translated into practical rules in the domain of vocabulary as follows:—

Prefer the familiar word to the far-fetched.
Prefer the concrete word to the abstract.
Prefer the single word to the circumlocution.
Prefer the short word to the long.
Prefer the Saxon word to the Romance.

Strunk was also mirroring the sentiment of one of America's most celebrated writers, Mark Twain. Their lives overlapped— Twain died in 1910, when Strunk was forty-one—and it's easy to guess that Strunk, with his taste for dry humor and plain, forceful writing, found Twain a companionable literary spirit. In a well-known essay, "Fenimore Cooper's Literary Offenses," Twain offered a few brief pointers useful to writers, with simplicity as the keystone. He advised that an author should:

Say what he is proposing to say, not merely come near it.

Use the right word, not its second cousin.

Eschew surplusage.

Not omit necessary details.

Avoid slovenliness of form.

Use good grammar.

Employ a simple and straightforward style.

An appreciative reader told White that his writing helps to assure her that the world is a rational place and gives her as much pleasure as listening to Bach.

Dear Mrs. _____

Thanks for a very kind and satisfying letter. I'm not sure about the world's being a rational place, but I must look up Bach and see what he's been up to.

Sincerely,
E. B. White

In a 2000 interview in *The New York Times,* talking about the evolution of simplicity in his own work, the composer and lyricist Stephen Sondheim touched the heart of the matter (and gave a nod to our man White). " 'Less is more' is a lesson learned with difficulty," Sondheim said. "As you get older, you pay more attention to it—that's why composers end up writing string quartets. . . . Reduction releases power. E. B. White may be my favorite American writer because of that."

FRANK MCCOURT
Faulkner once said of Hemingway that he never used a word that might send a reader to a dictionary. Hemingway responded, "Poor Faulkner. Does he really think big emotions come from big words?"

Reduction releases power. The point, then, of omitting needless words, of eschewing surplusage, of preferring the concrete word to the abstract, is not primarily to ensure that one's writing will be accessible to the greatest number of readers. That is an ancillary, almost accidental, blessing. The point of all this streamlining, in Sondheim's words, is the release of power—the creative and communicative power generated by the hard work of getting down to the essences of things. The effort to see clearly, think logically, and express oneself with precision leads the careful artist toward concision and simplicity, and, necessarily, to a greater concentration of force. "If you would be pungent, be brief," advised the poet Robert Southey, "for it is with words as with sunbeams—the more they are condensed, the deeper they burn." Generations of thinkers, writers, and artists have recognized the effect, and few have pursued it with such resolve and success as Thoreau, working by lamplight in his cabin in the woods, and E. B. White, leaning over his manual typewriter in the boathouse at the edge of the cove.

SIMPLICITY

"A sentence should contain no unnecessary words, a paragraph no unnecessary sentences, for the same reason that a drawing should have no unnecessary lines and a machine no unnecessary parts." William Strunk Jr.'s classic axiom is the first principle of clear and powerful prose, which is built from simple sentences and paragraphs. Simple, not simplistic: As Leonardo da Vinci is purported to have said, "Simplicity is the ultimate sophistication." The *New Yorker* writers Alec Wilkinson and Ian Frazier, masters of prose styles that are simultaneously simple and sophisticated, talk about simplicity in writing.

Alec Wilkinson says most of the work of simplifying happens in rewriting. "As William Maxwell used to say, 'You can't have the critic and the writer in the room at the same time.' So I try to get the words on the page first, before I then start to think about things like: Is this sentence too long? Does it need to be two sentences? Are these two sentences too abrupt? Do they need to be one sentence? That sort of thing. So one arrives at the finished product, which is what one hopes the world will embrace. I think it has something to do with what's companionable to one's nature, and how one feels one is going to make the best impression in the world. I don't think there's any point in going to some flamboyant personality and saying, 'Tone it down.' But even the flamboyant personalities—writers such as Tom Wolfe—even they have restricted themselves to a fairly straightforward approach. And in writers such as Maxwell or Joseph Mitchell or Hemingway, or even Virginia Woolf, who is much more ornate, there's a recognition that the rules of writing require that material be compressed when it's necessary, that not everything be examined at length and in detail; pacing is important. In the end, Henry James's remark of 'dramatize, dramatize, dramatize' is going to come down to 'simplify, simplify, simplify.' It's not sound advice to tell writers to 'complicate, complicate, complicate.' It doesn't work in mechanical things: When people build cars or other machines, they try to use the fewest number of moving parts because moving parts break. They're not thinking, How many moving parts can we put on this thing? It's a principle of nature, practically, an organic principle. Nature designs simply. And it's a principle that's congenial to writing because it's one of the fundamental ways in which the world functions.

"For all those reasons, any piece of writing that's too dense or too complicated, or that meanders and violates the rules that Strunk and White lay down, is going to be unsuccessful. Readers are going to have difficulty with it. A movie doesn't consist of all the scenes the director shot; it consists of those scenes that the editor and the director have decided are most effective. No one advises that, by being as complicated as you possibly can, as obscure, as difficult, as impenetrable, you will succeed. And it's important, too, to recognize how widely applicable those Strunk and White rules are, to look at who fits within them. James Joyce fits within them; Virginia Woolf fits; Hemingway fits. As Hemingway said, and as Strunk and White believed, most adjectives and adverbs are not necessary. But, that doesn't mean that in the hands of certain people they aren't used to great effect. Even so, I can't think of any admired writer—I'm not talking about people who sell books but anybody who's admired as a writer—whose work is flaccid and overstuffed."

Ian Frazier: "I think of simplicity as being related to the idea of cool. You have the experience in high school, if you're a guy who wants to impress girls, of trying to impress girls, and then seeing that the people who aren't trying are having vastly more success. As you get older, you see that many people who do very well in the world are people who let other people project things onto them and don't disturb the fantasy. They let things be projected on them. Mr. Shawn, *The New Yorker*'s former editor, was a very good example of that. There was a huge amount of energy focused on him, all these absolutely driven and desperate, hope-filled writers trying to do something, and they were focusing on this guy, Mr. Shawn, and he knew enough to keep his mouth shut. It reminds me of something I heard recently that Will Rogers said: 'Never miss an opportunity to shut up.'

"When you are trying to write as simply as you can, you're leaving plenty of comfort zone for the reader. A piece of writing doesn't really exist on the page—it exists between what's on the page and the reader. It's not all the way in the reader and it's not all the way on the page; it's in between. And when you have done things with the least amount of noise and effort, you give readers the easiest access to that middle zone. They get there and they can supply what's needed. It's very flattering to a reader's imagination; I don't mean flattering in a base way, but because it assumes the reader's imagination is powerful and that it needs not a whole lot to make a picture, to make a narrative. You give it enough to do that, and you don't choke it with all kinds of extraneous stuff that you're enjoying but the reader might not. This rule would immediately fall to the ground if you were to look at something like *Ulysses*. No rule in writing is absolute, including this one, I guess. But I suppose the basic thing is that you behave respectfully to the reader. You know where you're going, and you tell him where you're going without sending him running down a lot of false alleys."

6

As Elusive as a Rabbit

Do you think this dreadful little book
will ever settle down and stay quiet?

—E. B. WHITE

While the spirit of *The Elements of Style* has stood rocklike for a couple of generations, the book itself has not remained changeless, locked in decades-old amber. Since 1959, through multiple revisions and dozens of printings (twenty-five in the first edition alone), its contents have been refined, rearranged, expanded, trimmed, shaken, stirred, fixed, and occasionally nixed in response to the restless character of the English language—its tendency to jump the curb and travel off-road, snagging surprising new oddities in the underbrush and leaving outmoded scraps behind. Throughout the 1960s and 1970s, White and his Macmillan editors remained vigilant. Small fixes were dealt with between printings, and in the years before E. B. White's death in 1985, he undertook two major revisions—the second edition, published in 1972, and the third, in 1979.

As soon as the 1959 first edition was sent to the printer, both

White and Jack Case developed the habit of jotting down notes about possible changes for subsequent editions. In their effort to keep the book fresh and accurate, they drew on reviews, their own reading, and the continual flow of letters they received from the many vigilant readers who seemed to be inspecting the book with jeweler's loupes. In the summer of 1960, one such letter reached White—a good-natured jab at a flaw in *Elements*' treatment of syllabication, the dividing of words across line breaks. White forwarded the letter to Jack Case, with this note:

June 13, 1960

Dear Jack:

   Mr. Ginzburg seems to have a point here, and I don't know whether the fix has been made. Do you think this dreadful little book will ever settle down and stay quiet?
   Although not in good health I am in reasonably good spirits and am enjoying the spring, with a yellow warbler nesting in the honeysuckle bush by the garage door—which is spring enow for me.

Yrs,
Andy

Case responded, agreeing that the reader's point was a good one, and he mentioned that "one of these days" the book should be revised. He added, "To answer your question whether I think 'this dreadful little book' (first-year sales over 200,000 copies) 'will ever settle down and stay quiet,'—no, except for Chapter V, I don't. Because English won't."

Jack Case's unspecified "one of these days" was a long time coming, and it was a day that he himself would not live to see.

More than a decade would pass before work on the second edition got under way (and more than 2 million copies of the first edition of *The Elements of Style* would be sold before the publication of the second). The years between 1959 and 1972 were busy ones for the Whites. Katharine retired from *The New Yorker* in 1961, after her remarkable and groundbreaking thirty-five-year career at the magazine, but she was in poor health for much of the rest of her life. White's anxiety about his wife's well-being was continual through the sixties and seventies, and he endured physical and emotional ailments of his own, which were often exacerbated by his anxiety about Katharine. His literary output continued, however. He still wrote for *The New Yorker,* though at his own pace, and without weekly deadlines; a collection of his *New Yorker* pieces, *The Points of My Compass,* was published in 1962; and his third children's book, *The Trumpet of the Swan,* came out in 1970, the year he was honored with the Laura Ingalls Wilder Medal for his two previous children's books, *Stuart Little* and *Charlotte's Web.*

White had been busy, but the delay in getting around to the revision of *The Elements of Style* seemed also to have a hint of hesitation in it, possibly a reluctance to jump back into the roiling waters of English grammar and usage. The many small errors in the book that had come to light since the publication of the first edition—those either created or missed by Strunk, White, and Case, and those introduced inadvertently by printers and others—were disheartening to White, who, after receiving a letter from a reader concerning a particularly embarrassing gaffe in the first paragraph of Chapter V ("There is no . . . inflexible rules by which the young writer may shape his course") wrote to Case that he was going to "burn my typewriter and scatter the ashes over Lower Fifth Avenue." By 1970, it was clear that the book was in need of a thorough overhaul, and Jack Case prodded gently:

January 30, 1970

Dear Andy:

Congratulations on the Medal! It should go nicely on the front of that sweater. I take it this represents the complete and final surrender of the librarians to Stuart Little—I recall that it was touch and go there for a while—and I hope he is letting them keep their swords and mouse-nots.

So the secret is out—that "story book" is THE TRUMPET OF THE SWAN. And now that you have nothing to do except perhaps read a little proof, let's begin to consider the Augean stables of American English usage, and how THE ELEMENTS can be made an even more effective shovel than it now is.

I hope Mrs. White is having a better time of it. I myself am riding on pills, a cane, and the Penn-Central, which is as much a death-in-life [as] anyone needs.

Yours,
Jack

White agreed in principle, but it would be nearly another year and a half before he got down to business on the revision. And in the interim, on November 13, 1970, Jack Case, the editor who had landed *The Elements of Style* for Macmillan, who had championed both the book and its singular viewpoint among his colleagues and his academic customers, who had brought it to market with an energy and style all his own, and who had made a friend in E. B. White, passed away.

The second edition, and the third, would be shepherded to market by a young Macmillan editor, the aptly named Anthony English, a native of England and a graduate of Trinity College, Cambridge. Harry Cloudman made the introduction in a June

1971 letter to White and predicted that he would find English "bright and pleasant."

Tony English, in his first letter to White, broaching the subject of the second edition, expressed some trepidation at stepping into Jack Case's role; he was deferential and respectful of the book's legacy, but he was not shy about getting the business of revision under way, and he urged White to have the updated manuscript to him by November 1971—a short five months later. English forwarded to White his own suggestions for changes, lengthy commentary from three paid consultants (English professors), and Jack Case's own revision notes.

Dear Mr. _____

> *Thank you for your belated birthday wishes.*
> *Although my roots and my heart are in New England, I envy you moving to Bradenton. I like that warm salt sea water in November and in April, and if I have any luck I may try another visit this fall to Sarasota to take the baths.*
> *Good luck in your pursuit of English usage. It's as elusive as a rabbit.*
>
> *Yrs,*
> *E. B. White*

White began the revision in August, and his correspondence during the period shows his distaste for the job: "It's not the kind of work I find easy or pleasurable or both"; "I would much rather be sorting the dirty clothes"; "I'm still slugging away at a revision of 'The Elements of Style' for Macmillan. I hate the guts of English grammar." But he bore down on it and hit his deadline squarely, posting the revised manuscript to Tony English on November 12, 1971. The changes were wide-ranging and included the following:

- The combining of "A Note on This Book" (a prefatory statement about the book's origins in the 1959 edition) and the Introduction.
- A change in Chapter II, Rule 12 ("Use definite, specific, concrete language"). The excerpted example of admirably tangible prose was switched from a selection from Willa Cather's *My Ántonia* to a vivid scene of airplane passengers caught in a storm taken from John Cheever's "The Country Husband."
- A half page on the use of the hyphen added to Chapter III, "A Few Matters of Form."
- Additions to the list of reference books recommended at the beginning of Chapter IV, including *The American Heritage Dictionary,* Theodore Bernstein's *Watch Your Language,* and Fowler's *Dictionary of Modern English Usage.*
- The addition of many new words to Chapter IV, "Words and Expressions Commonly Misused" (including *aggravate, among-between, each and every one, finalize, flammable, hopefully, kudos, meaningful, nice, relevant,* and *utilize*) and the deletion of several (among them, *aforesaid, oftentimes-ofttimes,* and *phase*).
- The addition of a new paragraph to Chapter V, "An Approach to Style," one that would continue to require revision in subsequent editions—White's warning that writers be careful about spicing text with too many currently in-vogue words, because of their tendency to age quickly. The examples White cited were a lovely evocation of the bell-bottomed, turned-on, Pink-Floyded era in which the second edition updates were undertaken: *uptight, groovy, rap, hangup, vibes, copout,* and *dig.*

The second edition, at seventy-eight pages, was seven pages longer than the first.

One of the most substantial outside contributions to the second edition of *The Elements of Style,* and one that had come as a surprise to White, was made by a co-worker: Eleanor Gould Packard, *The New Yorker*'s "Grammarian." Like White, she had been hired by Harold Ross, and over the course of her fifty-four years at the magazine, "Miss Gould," as she was known in the office, hard-scrubbed the prose of some of the most famous nonfiction writers of the twentieth century. David Remnick, the magazine's current editor, writing on the occasion of her death in 2005, noted that she had "shaped the language of the magazine, always striving for a kind of Euclidean clarity—transparent, precise, muscular. It was an ideal that seemed to have not only syntactical but moral dimensions." Remnick wrote that Miss Gould "could find a solecism in a Stop sign." As White began working on the second edition, he wrote to Miss Gould to ask about some of the reference books currently favored at *The New Yorker* (for updating his introduction to Chapter IV). She responded with a long note telling White, in an admission she found somewhat embarrassing, that when the 1959 edition of *The Elements of Style* had first been published, she had marked up her copy, noting some errors and inconsistencies, primarily as an editorial reflex, but also with the possibility in mind of her work someday being useful for a revision. When White's reference-book questions had arrived and she'd learned of the upcoming revision, she had purchased the latest version of *Elements,* the twenty-fifth printing of the first edition, and compared it with the decade-old first printing in which she had made her marks. Most of the problems she had noted in the original printing were still there, and she offered to share her work with White. He gladly accepted the offer. As he later explained to Tony English:

There was hardly a page that she hadn't found to be riddled with error. Anyway, her marked copy was a guide to me in the fog-shrouded sea of grammar. She deserves some sort of life-saving medal. I'll try to send her a couple of mink-lined semicolons for Christmas.

Most of the errors Miss Gould had noted were mechanical ones—problems of consistency in the use of italics, punctuation, capitalization, and the like. Her long letters to White during the updating are bright and funny, bristling with the pointed grammatical sensibility for which she was known. They are also hand-written on unlined stationery, in a close but legible script. White apparently found her handwriting rough going; in the midst of the proceedings, he offered to make her the gift of a typewriter. She graciously but firmly declined the offer. For her help, Eleanor Gould Packard received a special acknowledgment in both the second and third editions of *The Elements of Style*.

The Elements of Style, 1972
The Elements of Style *by William Strunk Jr. and E. B. White. Copyright by Pearson Education Inc. Used by permission.*

ADAM GOPNIK

I grew up as the son of professors. My mother is a linguist, and my father is an English professor. And one of the little ironies of my own engagement with *The Elements of Style* is that both of my parents were extremely critical of any kind of prescriptive grammar. In other words, they both believed strongly, and still believe, that the nature of language is to change all the time and that any attempt to impose one set of language rules is always based on a fallacy—that is, that there is a right and a wrong way to write or speak— and that it simply prescribes somebody's arbitrary prefer- ences, the arbitrary preferences of one class of speakers, as though they were logical rules. And that happens to be true; from a scientific point of view, from a linguistic point of view, that's the case. The rules that Shakespeare wrote by are not the rules of *The Elements of Style,* they're not the rules of good grammar as we understand them, and so on. But, at the same time, when I started reading *New Yorker* stuff— when I started reading White and Thurber—I was drawn to the elements of *that* style.

The final typescript of the 1972 edition, in the White archive at Cornell, shows again the level of care taken with the manuscript by White and everyone at Macmillan. The red-pencil marks and comments of a thorough and thoughtful copy editor are an- swered in green pencil by White, with tact, firm common sense, and the occasional "Good catch!" And ever vigilant, here in his seventy-second year, he is still on the prowl for needless words:

a green squiggle deletes, for instance, the word *just* from "The word itself is just a tangle" (Chapter V, Rule 12), a sentence that had borne the bloat for more than ten years.

The completion of the second edition was a relief to White, and though there was a tremendous amount of media interest on the occasion of the revision—Macmillan fielded calls from all of the major networks and newsmagazines seeking out the author for interviews and personal appearances—White asked Tony English to do his best to block all interview requests. Though the mass of writers, then and now, might barter their grandchildren for a chance at that kind of publicity, for most of his life White had carefully avoided public speaking and the general folderol of authorial celebrity, and he was not about to change course at this late date. He also asked that English handle the inevitable influx of readers' suggestions and complaints by first acknowledging them and then filing copies in the Macmillan office before forwarding the correspondence to him. It was best, White reasoned, that the file of all the correspondence and proposed updates be kept in the Macmillan office. "With any luck," he told English, "I'll be dead before the time arrives for a third edition."

No such luck. Work on the next edition would begin just five years later. Tony English first raised the question in early 1977. In a three-page letter that's a masterful mix of lighthearted cajolery and editorial diplomacy, English approaches the topic as if he's about to poke a tiger with a stick.

January 11, 1977

Dear Mr. White:

You must have experienced, either at first hand or vicariously, almost every surprise the publishing world is capable of springing on an author. But editors are low, callous fellows who cannot resist practical stratagems or imagine that there is anything flat in setting a full bucket over the door and inviting the author to come in. I have a bucket over the door, but I'll set myself above my peers to the extent of giving you fair warning and leaving you to lift the latch or not according to your taste for a refreshing shower.

Can you be persuaded to give The Elements of Style *another face lift?*

To do the magnitude of that question justice, I should at least have spread the words out one at a time over fourteen pages, with the question mark standing alone on the last. . . .

Sincerely,
D. Anthony English

English's interest in a revision of *Elements* was being driven by changes in curricular needs. Teachers, he told White, had for several years been aware of a steady deterioration in the writing skills of college students. "Their reaction," he wrote, "has been to accept renewed responsibility to teach what is right as well as how to turn the mind inside out and discover the self," and writing programs were now abuzz about getting "back to basics" or, as English described it, "a wholesome return to the principles of *The Elements of Style.*" His suggestion was not that White should alter or delete anything already in the text but that the addition of a few key topics would go a long way toward making *Elements* a more complete tool for writing teachers of the day. Specifically, he hoped White might have more to say on subject-verb and pronoun-antecedent agreement, and on the dash and the colon. He also felt that a new raft of words and phrases stood ready for induction into Chapter IV ("Words and Expressions Commonly Misused"). "I should like to know," English concluded, "if there is any prospect of our having a fresh edge put on the old blade."

Tony English proposed to save White the trouble of wading into the third-edition revisions from scratch by spending a couple months roughing in the kinds of additions he envisioned for the book and then turning them over to White for his consideration, emendation, or rejection. English sent his suggested revisions to White in May 1977. He advised adding four new sections to Chapter I ("Elementary Rules of Usage"): Rule 7, on the use of the colon; Rule 8, concerning dashes; Rule 9, on subject-verb agreement; and Rule 10, on pronoun case. English recommended isolated tweaks in other chapters—including a section warning against the use of unnecessary auxiliaries and conditionals under Rule 15 (old Rule 11), Chapter II, and a paragraph about certain idiomatic uses of prepositions in Rule 19 (formerly 15), Chapter II. He had also crafted a section explaining and defending the convention of using the pronoun *he* to refer to antecedents of indeterminate gender. In delivering his recommended changes, he reiterated to White that his goal was to provide a starting point that might simplify White's task in the revision.

Shortly after White received Tony English's starter edit for the third revision, and before he had gotten down to work, his wife, Katharine, succumbed to congestive heart failure. She died on July 20, 1977. Their marriage, of almost forty-eight years, had been an unusually rich and companionable partnership, and the blow was a sharp one to White. After Katharine's passing, he was occupied by the pragmatic concerns of adjusting to life as a widower, and he spent a great deal of time replying to the correspondence and condolences that flowed in. This was in addition to the work of responding to the already overwhelming stream of letters that had been arriving from charmed readers of his *Letters of E. B. White*, which had been published to rave reviews just the year before.

Tony English let the matter of the revision rest. He did not raise the subject again until February 1978, when he sent White a politely probing letter to see if he was ready to begin working again on *Elements*. After passing his first winter on the farm without Katharine, White was indeed ready to again busy himself with his old friend Strunk. He worked steadily on the revision and delivered the finished manuscript to English in late March. In addition to the four new rules in Chapter I suggested by English, the list of "Words and Expressions Commonly Misused" grew to include new offenders, such as *currently, facility, insightful, -ize, offputting, ongoing,* and *secondly* (and lost *kudos, me, none, relevant,* and *whom*). The hipster lingo in Chapter V gained *ripoff, dude,* and *funky,* and gave up *groovy, hangup,* and *dig.*

The third-edition effort in the matter of *he* and *she* was a nod to the times. Sensitivity to perceived gender bias, particularly in educational texts, was on the rise. Feminist critics had begun pressing both White and Macmillan to make broad changes to the gender viewpoint of *Elements* by purging the book of its male-centric language; by drawing on more women writers for its literary examples; and by incorporating more images of strong, self-directed women in the book's examples and dissociating them from the dreary domestic tropes that they claimed were symbols of women's oppression—the ironing board, the dishwasher, the children underfoot. Critics ached to liberate and empower the fictional women who showed up in the text, women who came across as weak and irresolute or shackled by male notions of propriety and worth, women such as Chloë, of Chapter IV, who appears in the discussion of *like* and *as,* and who "smells good, as a pretty girl should." Textbooks, it was said, should not perpetuate sex-biased stereotypes or turn a blind eye to patriarchal chauvinism, such as in presuming to recommend how a young woman, pretty or otherwise, ought to smell.

Macmillan was feeling some pressure on the gender issue from its academic market, but the company was also disinclined to meddle with the successful, if idiosyncratic, voice of its bestseller. And unlike many other student writing texts, *The Elements of Style,* besides being a pragmatic guide to better writing, also happened to be a work of art that had been fine-tuned by one

of America's most respected and beloved writers. The thought at
Macmillan was that, as such, it had the right, perhaps the duty,
to stand apart from the general run of textbooks. White's own
attitude toward the squall appears to have been one of bemused
sympathy, but with little inclination to appease critics by making
what seemed like contrived gestures aimed at redressing supposed linguistic slights. The language would change, or not, in its
own good time, and *The Elements of Style* would stand or fall on
its merits. White doubtless foresaw the day when a broader adjustment to cultural and pedagogical trends would be required if
the book were to retain its usefulness and popularity, but on his
watch, *The Elements of Style* would continue to employ the tone,
idiom, and resolutely gender-complacent pronouns of the men
who had created it.

Dear Mr. _____

    *I share your concern but am not optimistic about the
outcome of the battle. The girls are fighting with a fury born
of centuries of oppression, and I don't think they'll stop till
they get the "men" out of "menopause" and "menstruation."
Even a "menagerie," if it houses any female creatures, will
feel the weight of their displeasure.*

    Good luck, swordsperson! Fight on!

                    Yrs,
                    E. B. White

P.S. See p. 60, Third Edition, THE ELEMENTS OF STYLE.

Since White and Macmillan were in agreement, the gender tinkering on the third edition was minimal. It included the introduction, in the examples, of a few new women in positions of authority, or at least portrayed in nondomestic situations, women such as Rachel Simonds, Attorney, and Jane, a job applicant. The excerpt meant to exemplify writing that is "specific and concrete" was changed from John Cheever's white-knuckle flight to a selection from Jean Stafford's short story "In the Zoo." But the ironing board and dishwasher remained, as did the attractive and fragrant Chloë.

The question of *he* and *she* had been handled summarily, and similarly, in the 1918, 1959, and 1972 editions, under the "They" entry in Chapter IV ("Words and Expressions Commonly Misused"): When searching for a pronoun to pair with an antecedent such as *anybody, any one, somebody,* or *some one,* both Strunk and White had advised: "Use *he* . . . unless the antecedent is or must be feminine." The 1979 edition's treatment of *he* and *she*

The Elements of Style, 1979
The Elements of Style *by William Strunk Jr. and E. B. White. Copyright by Pearson Education Inc. Used by permission.*

did not give much ground, but instead mounted a defense of the common usage. It was explained as a historical, practical construction with "no pejorative connotation." A sample of prose (a Somerset Maugham paragraph) was altered to show the convoluted, nonsensical result of substituting every *he* with *he or she,* every *his* with *his or her.* An alternative approach, White and English suggested, might be to pluralize all potentially trouble-some nouns, allowing the writer to fall back on *they,* thus avoid-ing the pronominal sex choice. But, they warned, "you may find your prose sounding general and diffuse as a result."

A reader asked White whether he or Strunk had composed the paragraph about *he* and *she,* and inquired about the re-numbering of some of the rules.

Dear Mr. _____

    Neither Strunk nor I composed the paragraph about the pronoun "he." My editor at Macmillan, a fellow named D. Anthony English, dreamed it up. He sent it to me when the Third Edition was in the making, and I grabbed it without a moment's hesitation.

    The companion passage in the First Edition was presumably a collaboration: Strunk plus me. I've forgotten.

    In the Second Edition, "Use definite, specific, concrete language" is Rule 12.

    Next question.

                    Yrs,
                    E. B. White

The first printing of the third edition of *The Elements of Style* was off the presses by December 1978, though it bears a 1979 copyright date. Like the second edition, the third was seven pages longer than its predecessor, weighing in at eighty-five pages. The little book blew into bookstores and just as quickly blew back out again. By July 1979, it had sold more than 300,000 copies, a half-year total that was higher than the best full-year sales of either the first or the second edition. The third edition was eventually enhanced by the addition of an index—a feature that readers and teachers had been requesting since the first edition. In January 1981, a teacher offered Tony English an index he had made for his own classroom use. White and English decided to incorporate it into the book, it was edited at Macmillan, and it debuted in the seventh printing of the third edition, in September 1981. The index added yet another seven pages to the total, bringing the book to a still-svelte ninety-two pages.

In 1984, the year before White's death, Tony English wrote to him, raising the possibility of a fourth edition. White's reaction to the idea is not recorded. He died in October 1985, and the 1979 third edition of *The Elements of Style* was the last to be published with his oversight.

In the years following the release of the third edition, the publishing home of *The Elements of Style* shifted, as the Macmillan Company navigated through a variety of corporate mergers and splits. Today it is published by Longman, an imprint of Pearson Higher Education. In the late 1990s, almost twenty years after the book's last revision, the editors at Longman themselves decided to enter the fray by publishing a revised fourth edition of *The Elements of Style*. The goal was to ensure the book's relevance for today's students, who still make up the largest single group of its readers, and to align the book with modern guidelines for gender-neutral language in textbooks.

By the time of White's death, the book had sold millions

of copies, and it was widely regarded as a modern classic, one of the most successful and iconic textbooks ever published. As delicate as the job of updating *The Elements of Style* had been during White's lifetime, the idea of tinkering with the revered text without his oversight might have struck many of the faithful as tantamount to heresy. No matter how it turned out, there was no way the fourth-edition update was going to please everyone. On its publication, late in 1999, reviews were varied. The *San Francisco Chronicle* welcomed it. ("[It] completely eliminates some hopelessly dated views of gender roles. White's own elegant style shines through.") *The Wall Street Journal* expressed doubts about the new edition's attention to "gender correctness" and its extra heft (the book is now 105 pages long). *The Boston Globe* felt that not enough had been done to pull *Elements* into the present ("If White had been around to help, I suspect he would have revised more energetically"). The broad range of critical reaction seemed to indicate that Longman had struck just about the right balance of renovation and conservation.

The publisher had justifiably high hopes for the fourth edition. On the occasion of its publication, Bill Barke, then president of Allyn & Bacon, a Longman sister imprint, told *Publishers Weekly* that, before the 1999 update, *The Elements of Style* had been selling "about 230,000 copies a year without even trying." The company expected, he said, to sell some 500,000 copies of the new edition before the end of 2000 and eventually fall back to a steady 300,000 copies annually.

From the point of view of the publisher, the fourth-edition revision was a clear necessity. "The majority of sales for *The Elements of Style* are to students taking writing courses," says Joseph Opiela, Senior Vice President and Publisher at Longman. "In 1997, we surveyed college writing instructors to ask for feedback about the book as a classroom text and writing reference. Responses indicated that students would benefit from some carefully chosen revisions. For instance, the list of reference works on page 39 was updated, the dates in the examples on page 35 were changed, and some examples throughout were changed to replace older authors with contemporary ones. While the book had generally aged well, we realized that some updating would keep it fresh and relevant. Of course, the specific advice about grammar, style, and writing throughout continued to be valid and worthwhile. However, many of the examples were from a different era and the use of pronouns in the book was not in accord with the current recommendations of the National Council of Teachers of English (NCTE). While we did not want to compromise any of the subtle humor in these examples, we updated some to be more modern and inclusive, and revised individual sentences to adhere to the NCTE guidelines on the use of pronouns."

The fourth edition of *The Elements of Style* introduces several new components—a foreword from White's stepson, Roger Angell, a brief afterword by Charles Osgood, and a glossary. The structure and argument of the book, however, remain largely unchanged. "Words and Expressions Commonly Misused" gained one entry, "care less," and the discussion of *they* was updated to include current thinking on the matter of *he* and *she* and now offers several alternatives for the writer wishing to impart a more modern, egalitarian sensibility to her pronouns. The gender-related updating of the text was thorough, with a great deal more *her*ing and *she*ing and the addition of more females to the book's many examples. Women new to the fourth edition of *Elements* include Sappho, Jane Austen, Emily Dickinson, Edith Wharton, and Molly Bloom. Mary Shelley nudges out Robert Louis Stevenson, Marianne Moore displaces E. A. Robinson, Plath supplants Keats, and William Wordsworth gives way to Toni Morrison. The troublesome Chloë has been dealt with, deftly, by age regression;

she now "smells good, as a baby should." The weary mother with the ironing board and the houseful of children is gone. The dishwasher remains, but *he,* not *she,* is using it.

Joseph Opiela says his editorial team was careful to maintain the tone and voice of both authors. "We worked hard to keep the authorial voices of Strunk and White intact," he says. "The vast majority of their narrative remains untouched. Where it was necessary to revise, care was taken not to change meaning or tone. In all cases, our effort was to change wording as little as possible and still accomplish our goals. We were guided every step of the way by our goal to remain as true as possible to the voice and tone of both White and Strunk. We made only the minimal changes we considered important to keep the book viable as a writing guide for today's classrooms."

The White family was involved with the updating. "A team of editors under my direction made suggestions for revisions to examples and pronoun use," says Opiela. "We consolidated those suggestions and prepared a draft manuscript with the particular changes that we thought were appropriate and did not compromise the authors' voice. We shared that manuscript with Allene White [E. B. White's daughter-in-law] and received approval before going ahead with it. Roger Angell also saw the manuscript before publication."

Allene White, speaking to a *New York Times* reporter on the occasion of the new edition's release, said that the publisher's sending the manuscript to the White family had been "like sending raw meat to a cage of lions. . . . When push comes to shove, we shove so well, we make so much noise. Essentially it now has the same point of view as Mr. White had."

It's easy enough for a devotee weaned on the third edition to get a little blue about all this updating, particularly since E. B. White no longer has a hand in the game. I'm happy enough for

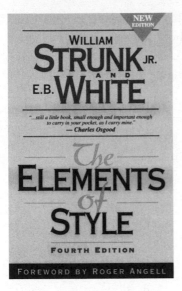

The Elements of Style, 1999

The Elements of Style *by William Strunk Jr. and E. B. White. Copyright by Pearson Education Inc. Used by permission.*

Dickinson, Austen, Plath, and the rest, but sometimes I miss the banished boys: Robinson, Maugham, Fowles, Pliny the Younger, and others. I try to imagine what E. B. White might have to say about the insertion of computers and word processing into his Chapter V essay. As to Chloë: I like babies, but I'm also in favor of pretty girls who smell good. But the Longman editors made the right decision, the only decision they could have made, and they handled it neatly. All the essentials, the elements, are still there in the fourth edition, and they're delivered with the same voice and tone as ever. It had simply become necessary once again, in the words originally expressed by Jack Case, to "saw off bits of outdated scroll work here and there." Most important, the revisions have had the effect of preserving the commercial appeal of *The Elements of Style,* thereby assuring its future as a living agent of culture rather than a museum piece. And if dispelling some of the book's clubbishness—and that's about what it amounts to, more like breaking up a poker game than, say, revising the Roman Catholic liturgy—if that's the price we are to pay for keeping Strunk, White, and the sharp good sense of *The Elements of Style* viable for a new generation of students and writers, it's a bargain.

7

The Self Escaping

You can say anything that comes into your head, never forget that.

—E. B. WHITE

In the summer of 1935, E. B. White received a letter from Will Strunk written on stationery from the Hollywood-Roosevelt Hotel in Hollywood, California. His old friend was in high spirits.

July 19, 1935

Dear Andy:

. . . I am writing to tell you that I am in pix and enjoying it greatly. I am doing advisory work for M.-G.-M. on their forthcoming Romeo and Juliet. All I will say is that the dialogue will be exclusively from Shakespeare's text, that the scene will be in Verona, and that they will not live happily ever after. . . .

Romeo and Juliet is going to be a great picture, but you will learn about that from the Publicity and Advertising Departments. . . .

Best regards as ever,
W. S. Jr

The movie was being produced by Irving Thalberg, the "boy wonder" responsible for some of classic Hollywood's most successful films, from *A Night at the Opera* to *Mutiny on the Bounty*. Thalberg intended to create the most authentic version of *Romeo and Juliet* yet attempted—overlooking the strain on verisimilitude introduced by the casting of his thirty-four-year-old wife, Norma Shearer, as the fourteen-year-old virgin, Juliet, and Leslie Howard, at forty-two, as Romeo—and he recruited William Strunk Jr. as a technical adviser for the film, on a recommendation from the Folger Shakespeare Library in Washington, D.C.

Early negotiations with Strunk, via long-distance telephone, stalled when Thalberg was told that the professor had asked for $400 a week. Thalberg's story editor, Samuel Marx, happened to be on the East Coast at the time, scouting stories and writers, and the producer asked him to contact Strunk and try to talk him down to the preferred rate of $150 a week. "If necessary," Thalberg told Marx, "give him two hundred. After all, he is special." Marx phoned Ithaca from New York City, and Strunk asked him to talk to the dean, who would negotiate in his stead. The dean insisted that a $400 salary was standard for such work, and that a portion of the money would be used to pay other teachers who would be needed to handle Strunk's classes while he was engaged on the film. Marx balked at the request and counteroffered $200. The dean turned it down, explaining, "I assure you many professors *are* paid four hundred dollars a month!" Marx was dumbfounded: Strunk and the dean had been pursuing a monthly, not a weekly, fee. They quickly settled on Thalberg's original figure of $150 per week.

Strunk took a six-week leave of absence from Cornell and went on his first visit to California. At the end of six weeks, the producers exercised their option to keep him on for an addi-

THOMAS E. HULL
MANAGING DIRECTOR

HOLLYWOOD·ROOSEVELT HOTEL

HOLLYWOOD
CALIFORNIA

July 19, 1935.

Dear Andy:

I rang you up the night of July 4, with little hope, I admit, of finding you in New York. Got your address now, after this delay, I am writing to tell you that I am in pix and enjoying it greatly. I am doing advisory work for M-G-M on their forthcoming Romeo and Juliet. All I will say is that the dialogue will be exclusively from Shakespeare's text, that the scene will be in Verona, and that they will not live happily ever after.

Sent the New Yorker a clipping from an L.A. paper the other day; it may or may not have amused them: "The pastor's subject in the morning will be, How to End the Depression; in the evening, Oh, for the Life of a Fireman!" This of course was Aimee, but her name was not in that sentence, so that it could be quoted, if they saw fit, without giving her any unpaid advertising.

Romeo and Juliet is going to be a great picture, but you will learn about that from the Publicity and Advertising Departments.

Please present my best compliments to Mrs. White.

Best regards as well,

W.S.Jr.

Strunk wrote to White from Hollywood.

Used by permission of Allene White and the estate of E. B. White.

Dear Miss _____

    The dash didn't get into the book, but it seems to get into my writing now and then—the way things do. As for three dots . . .

    Everybody is confused about "I were," but if I were you, I wouldn't let it worry me. It belongs to the subjunctive mood.

    I say eether, *rather than* eyether. *But you can say anything that comes into your head, never forget that.*

                Sincerely,
                E. B. White

tional four weeks. This pattern continued, and Strunk eventually requested leave for the remainder of the term, and then for the entire year. A contemporary newspaper report from Hollywood notes that "every time someone has thrown a farewell party for him, the studio has signed him for an additional few weeks and he has had to have his leave of absence extended. Not altogether unwillingly."

Just two years away from retirement after nearly a half century in the college classroom, Will Strunk was having a grand time in Hollywood. He wrote to friends back home, letting them know about the class of people he was now hobnobbing with. He socialized with the film's cast, which, in addition to Shearer and Howard, included Basil Rathbone and John Barrymore, and attended parties where he met other celebrities, among them Jean Harlow, Tallulah Bankhead, and Joan Crawford. He lunched with the Thalbergs and dined at the Trocadero.

THOMAS KUNKEL

You have to let your voice evolve. As a young writer, you will probably tend to mimic writers you like, but eventually your own voice will emerge into your own style. And that is as true today as ever, and White would be the first to say that that's the way it should be. He would say we don't need more writers out there who sound like E. B. White. I think anybody who thinks of *The Elements of Style* as dogmatic is not reading it right.

Strunk joked that he had come to Hollywood "to protect the rights of the late William Shakespeare," and by all indications he was pleased with the result and proud to have contributed to a film that was both a commercial and an artistic success. He was well liked by the cast, crew, and production team, who regarded him as both a curiosity and a quintessential example of his breed. He was known around the MGM lot as "the professor," and articles in the Hollywood press and elsewhere enjoyed the fish-out-of-water aspect of the story. *The New York Times*' Hollywood correspondent wrote,

It is possible that Dr. Strunk is as startled by the industry as the industry is by him. . . . Academicians have never been popular with the town. . . . But Dr. Strunk, amiable, shrewd, seemingly bewildered, has molded the production so that, he believes, the most ardent student of Shakespeare will not only find no fault but will applaud. He found that a director or a producer is no harder to handle than a freshman, if you know how.

Part of the fun was that Strunk looked as though he'd been delivered to the set from MGM's casting department. Photographs taken during his Hollywood sojourn show him invariably done up in a three-piece suit and tie, hair carefully parted and pressed into place, round wire-rim spectacles shining. He was so convincing a professor that he was asked to consider a role in a Metro B production called *We Went to College*. He declined the offer. But Strunk relished his year in Hollywood, and he made a prediction for the *Times* writer:

> Dr. Strunk says that when he returns to Cornell he will carry an alarm clock that will ring when he has talked about Hollywood for fifteen minutes. He will fine himself a dollar, he says, every time he introduces the subject of Hollywood into conversation. "But if someone else brings the matter up, Heaven help him. He will have asked for it," he threatens.

It turns out he wasn't kidding. On his return to Ithaca, Strunk lectured at Cornell about his experience in the movies and talked about it with anyone who would listen, in or out of class. The starstruck professor made his Hollywood exploits so frequent a subject of conversation that at least one member of the family, his son Oliver, another professor from central casting, grew slightly embarrassed for him, as he felt his father was letting the Tinseltown experience overshadow a career filled with more substantial scholarly contributions.

The image of William Strunk working in the movie business is delightfully incongruous: Picture him scribbling notes on script pages poolside at the Hollywood-Roosevelt, eyes narrowed in the sunlight, collar button undone and tie pulled loose, a cool drink at one elbow and a telephone at the other. And after nearly a half century of *Mr. Chips*ing it at Cornell, he must have

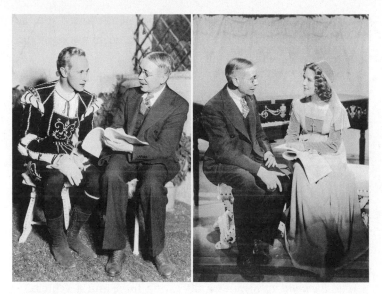

Romeo and Juliet and Strunk

relished the opportunity for this mild fling on his way out. I admire his readiness to brook some blushing within the family and, no doubt, occasional jibes from Cornell colleagues left behind to slog through another winter on the hill while he enjoyed the pools, palms, sun- and star-shine of Southern California. There is no indication that Strunk himself ever regretted his time in Hollywood, and if his enthusiasm for the project tested the bounds of Ivy League propriety, he regarded the work as an opportunity to help bring his beloved Shakespeare to a wider audience. He was also impressed by the manifold dramatic advantages offered by film over the live stage. "Film is an excellent medium in which to present Shakespeare," he told *The New York Times*. "The continuity of plot is more natural. Stage audiences are accustomed to listening, but picture audiences want to see things happen. In this the narrative has been resolved into action. The limitations of the stage necessitated many omissions that can be restored in the film."

The satisfactions, both academic and personal, that Strunk found in his work for Thalberg illustrate another core truth of *The Elements of Style*: that the point of art—the goal, in fact, of any creative undertaking—is the discovery and liberation of the voice, the self. While there is every reason to believe Strunk was happy in his academic career, it's also clear that during his year in Hollywood, working closely and intensively with the creative team on *Romeo and Juliet,* he found a new avenue of self-expression and perhaps even a new aspect of his character, an aspect that wasn't afraid to dial the scholarly reserve back a notch and have a go at a worthy slice of classi-pop culture.

The Elements of Style as a liberating force and a vehicle for self-discovery is an aspect of the book that often goes unnoticed by its detractors. But critics who see *Elements* as an appeal to conservatism and propriety—dusty admonitions from a couple of old-timers about staying within the lines, following the rules, and going no further—are missing one of the book's key points. *The Elements of Style* is not a destination; it's a springboard. And as much as some critics might decry both authors as hidebound "prescriptivists," Strunk and White knew well and, in fact, made clear within the pages of *The Elements of Style,* that rules don't make writers any more than scales make musicians. But, as with songs and scales, good writing makes sense only in relation to the rules, whether that relationship is expressed by adhering to them, by dancing with them, or by occasionally walking away from them. In his introduction to the 1918 edition, Strunk stated the axiom:

It is an old observation that the best writers sometimes disregard the rules of rhetoric. When they do so, however, the reader will usually find in the sentence some compensating merit, attained at the cost of the violation. Unless he is certain of doing as well, he will probably do best to follow the rules. After he has learned, by their guidance, to write plain English adequate for everyday uses, let him look, for the secrets of style, to the study of the masters of literature.

The last line turned out to be prophetic. The following year, Strunk would have just such a master of literature studying in his own classroom, and the same student, forty years on, would bring a new dimension to *The Elements of Style* by adding his own "secrets of style" in Chapter V, "An Approach to Style." White explains in the introduction to *Elements* that Chapter V sets forth "my own prejudices, my notions of error, my articles of faith." The chapter works as a counterbalance, broadening the discussion and encouraging writers to think about style, as White put it, "in its broader meaning . . . in the sense of what is distinguished and distinguishing." The essay is classic White: a thoughtful but pragmatic meditation, lithe and springy, brushed with humor, that circles and eventually alights on a handful of sensible truths about how writers might achieve a style and voice all their own. If Strunk had provided guidance for writing "plain English adequate for everyday uses," White's greatest contribution was to infuse the book with the spirit of the artist and provide an inspiring yet practical perspective about life on the other side of the rules. Chapter V introduced a level of nuance to *The Elements of Style* that Strunk, with his more immediately utilitarian goal (cleaner student papers) in mind, had chosen not to develop. Since White's experience was as a practitioner rather than as a teacher, he was uniquely equipped to champion his professor's objective approach to right and wrong while at the same time exploring the subjective mysteries of the writer's art and the subtleties of discovering voice, style, and the writer's "self."

Dear Mr. _____

It comes down to the meaning of "needless." Often a word can be removed without destroying the structure of a sentence, but that does not necessarily mean that the word is needless or that the sentence has gained by its removal.

If you were to put a narrow construction on the word "needless," you would have to remove tens of thousands of words from Shakespeare, who seldom said anything in six words that could be said in twenty. Writing is not an exercise in excision, it's a journey into sound. How about "tomorrow and tomorrow and tomorrow"? One tomorrow would suffice, but it's the other two that have made the thing immortal.

Thank you, thank you, thank you for your letter.

Yrs,
E. B. White

Readers who skim the headings in Chapter V ("Place yourself in the background," "Write with nouns and verbs," "Avoid fancy words," "Be clear," and the rest) and read no further might mistake it for a simple, even simplistic, continuation of Strunk's rules-focused theme. But "An Approach to Style" is neither simplistic nor a rigid prescription for how to write. The ideas developed in the essay are, in White's words, "mere gentle reminders" about how to clear the canvas so that style, the writer's voice on the page, can emerge. In the philosophical heart of Chapter V, its third paragraph, White explains his conception of style and its relation to the writer:

Style is an increment in writing. When we speak of Fitzgerald's style, we don't mean his command of the relative pronoun, we mean the sound his words make on paper. Every writer, by the way he uses the language, reveals something of his spirit, his habits, his capacities, his bias. This is inevitable as well as enjoyable. All writing is communication; creative writing is communication through revelation—it is the Self escaping into the open. No writer long remains incognito.

Style in this sense, White admits, is a mystery, an essentially organic development of the writer's art that, like happiness, cannot be approached head-on but can only be achieved as a by-product of aiming to produce work that's clear, natural, plain, and honest. But there are positive, tangible steps the hopeful writer can take, and the twenty-one "rules" that make up the rest of Chapter V guide White's writing readers along the path toward self-discovery and self-revelation. The secret, from White's point of view, largely comes down to clearing away the excess and, most important, being yourself. The advice might have sounded glib coming from any other source, but White was one of literature's strongest champions of individualism and self-determination, and though he struggled all his life with self-doubt, suffered occasional depressive episodes, nurtured a lush garden of neuroses, and could occasionally be mousier than his mouse-boy hero, Stuart Little, he was also more doggedly himself than most people have the nerve or stamina to be. He agreed with Strunk's contention that young and aspiring writers must pass through the gauntlet of instruction in the rules and familiarize themselves with the traditions and standards of plain English style, but he readily admitted that he wrote mostly "by ear"; the close parsing of grammar was not usually a conscious part of his writing process. And contrary to the claims of some *Elements* critics that White "didn't follow his own rules," it bears pointing out that the advice to be yourself; to experiment freely; and to trust your ear as the final arbiter of style, even, if necessary, at the expense of grammatical correctness, is all right there in Chapter V. Take another look.

NICHOLSON BAKER

The page is such a beautiful thing, and we all understand it. There's some white space at the top, then you start off and you're motoring along on a nice, long, straight stretch of highway, and it's a beautiful thing. Part of the fundamental pleasure of writing and of reading is that you really can't have two words side by side—everything has to be on the same string. Sometimes I'm driven to despair by the difficulty of that; other times it delights me. I like the idea of outlining things, framing things, of looking through a viewfinder and allowing its edges to define what you have to think about. Or staring at a chunk of turf until you begin to see all the creatures hopping around in there. That's what's so beautiful about E. B. White's pieces: He took a scrap of news, something seemingly random, and made it central by writing a square of words around it as a frame.

In a move that feels like the textual equivalent of an Escher point-of-view flip, Chapter V gently pivots the reader, placing him in right relation to the rules. From this new vantage point, he can look back over the book's first four chapters as over a stretch of country road traversed. Strunk's rules were an integral leg of the excursion, but they were only the first leg. And if they seem to have left the traveler facing something of a wall, White's essay dispels any misgivings. The wall is lower than it appears, and it's the simplest thing in the world to take the short step over it and move out into other landscapes.

White struggled with the composition of Chapter V. On re-reading it after having first turned it in to Jack Case, he confessed to Case that "it left me with a cold feeling of having failed." He felt that perhaps the introductory section of the essay (which, in that early incarnation, had begun with the "Style is an incre-ment in writing" paragraph) should be reduced, bringing the reader into the "rules" section more quickly. Case told White that he wasn't sure shorter was the answer; maybe the introductory portion should be longer, "a somewhat slower cast while you are getting out line." With that suggestion, Case bowed out. "You'll get it the way you want it," he told White. The final arrangement of Chapter V seems inevitable. White did lengthen the introduc-tion; it now unfolds over four pages, setting the stage for the chapter's twenty-one "gentle reminders" by inviting readers to think about the mystery of style, its integral relation to personal-ity, and the most helpful attitudes and expectations to bring to the job.

In his correspondence with *Elements* readers—many of whom seemed mired in a kind of grammatical scrupulosity—White was devoted to further expounding and promoting the liberating spirit of Chapter V. The care and frankness with which he answered these troubled correspondents offer strong evidence of his belief in his "approach to style" and show the responsibil-ity he felt to make himself clear on the point.

In the late 1970s, one overwrought reader wrote to ask for help with the "truly paralyzing confusion" that had taken hold of his life because of Rule 6, Strunk's admonition about the use and punctuation of sentence fragments. The question of punctuating fragments had become an obsession for this reader, and though it seems at first that he's having a bit of fun with White, it's soon clear that the letter is no hoax—he is suffering genuine, near-crippling mental anguish. He even included a check, offering to pay for White's "counseling." White's response, written just as work was about to get under way on the third revision of *The Elements of Style,* is indicative of at least two things: his great regard for his readers, and his ultimate confidence in the writer's ear.

Dear Mr. _____

Although I'm not equipped to deal with emotional disorders, I am *equipped to suggest to a writer what writing is all about. Writing is saying what you feel like saying in the way you feel like saying it. There are no* rules *of writing (who could possibly invent them?) there are only guidelines, and the guidelines can, and should be, chucked out of the window whenever they get in your way or in your hair. I have never paid the slightest attention to "The Elements of Style" when I was busy writing something.*

Having delivered myself of a preamble, I'll get on to your three questions:

1. *You are right.*
2. *You are right—I agree. Broken sentences are almost as frequent in dialogue as complete sentences. For all I know, they are* more *frequent.*
3. *Broken sentences don't need any justification if the writer happens to want to employ them. Mr. Strunk, although an orthodox man, was also a flexible man—as becomes any man who is essentially humorous. As you say in your letter, many skilled professional writers make frequent use of broken sentences. Strunk was flinging out his directives*

at the young, at the inexperienced, in short at his students.
He did use the word "rule", but he would have been the first
to deny (as indeed he did deny in the text) that a rule is not
for breaking. Nothing in the book is intended to "chastize"
anybody. If the book inhibits you, or constrains you, you
should build a bonfire and throw the book into the flames.

I was sorry I was unable to answer your first letter—it came
just after the death of my wife. I think my stepson, Roger Angell,
who is an accomplished writer, gave you the right answers, and
I agree with everything he said in his letter. I have been through
hard times myself with my head and my emotions, and I know
the torture that they can cause. But I have discovered that it is
possible to stay afloat and to get on top of the small and surprising
things that bother the head.

I suspect that you should disentangle yourself from the
so-called rules of grammar and style and get back to writing, if
writing is what you like to do. A surgeon, before he cuts someone,
has to know quite a bit about the intricacies of the human body;
but when he gets in there, with his knife, he has to make his
own way along. It is the same with a writer. There is always the
temptation to use something as a diversion or a device, to delay
the hard business of writing by putting up a handy obstacle. If
you have subconsciously put up an obstacle for yourself, only you
can knock it down. I can't knock it down for you, however much I
would like to do so.

But I send you my best wishes and will hope that you can put
"Rule 6" where it belongs—behind you.

I am returning your check, as I cannot accept payment for
counselling. I am not a counsellor.

Sincerely,
E. B. White

VOICE

For fifty years, E. B. White's contribution to *The Elements of Style* has coached writers on the post-Strunkian concern of bringing their authentic "selves" out into the open and creating a real voice on the page. The writers I interviewed had much to say about the work of finding and expressing their own voices as writers. We talked about E. B. White's observation that creative writing "is the Self escaping into the open," and about their own processes of self-discovery and achieving authenticity in their work.

Frank McCourt: "For me, it was the experience of the classroom. I wrote about this in *Teacher Man*. Kids asked me questions about my life, not because of their sincere interest, but because they were trying to get me away from any lesson I might be planning. So they'd ask me questions about my life, which I put no value on—my life, that is. But they seemed to find it interesting. This goes all the way back to my early days in the early sixties. And I would tell these stories and they would sit there, I wouldn't say with *rapt* attention, but somewhat interested, because I was a kind of exotic bloom, being Irish and not being of the general run of graduates from around city schools.

"Well, I was telling these stories, and a class in fall term would tell kids in the incoming class in the springtime, and they'd say, 'Aw, tell us the story about this . . . and tell us the story about that,' and I began to enjoy it. I began to enjoy the development of certain stories. For instance, in *Angela's Ashes* I wrote how I had a job as a writer for a moneylender, writing threatening letters to her clients, which I enjoyed, even though these clients were my own people in the back lanes of Limerick. And that story became more and more and more refined—Strunk would have enjoyed it because I got rid of all unnecessary words, phrases, and so on. So when I came to write it, it was already written. When I sat down that one morning in the little house in Pennsylvania, I just wrote it the way I had recited it in the classroom. And that comes from an oral tradition.

"Most of Irish tradition is oral anyway. The general populace didn't have paper, pens, quills, ink. The scarcity of paper when I was growing up—it's hard for Americans to believe this, or to understand. We didn't have writing materials. I used to write on the backs of paper bags, old wallpaper, anything at hand. So to come over here and find the endless supply of paper, that was absolutely luxurious. But because of that scarcity, everything was passed down and you had to have a memory. People are not going to listen to you, sitting around the farmhouse fire, if you're discursive and full of shit. They want you to get to the point. I learned that in the classroom, and that's how I tried to write.

"I think something miraculous happened in the writing of *Angela's Ashes*. I wrote about nineteen pages on my mother and father coming over from Ireland and meeting in New York—how they met, and how there was an encounter, and how I was born. Then I said, now tomorrow (I made a note to myself on the left-hand page) I'm going to start with my earliest memories. And I started writing sentences from my earliest memory that had to do with being on a seesaw in Brooklyn. And I just put it down; I wrote it from the point of view of a three-and-a-half-year-old, and that requires, demands, simplicity, and I was on my way with that. I didn't know this was going to happen, but childhood demands clarity, so from the age of four to the age of nineteen, I guess I moved along, becoming *slightly* more sophisticated."

So once you had this down on paper, it didn't take much fiddling then—it was all there?

"Yeah, it was there. And it was *almost* easy, but not really. I used to tell the kids something that Richard Brinsley Sheridan said, that easy writing is vile hard reading. And I always had that in mind. I'd go back, I would write pages and pages and then look at them and say, 'What shit is this?' and throw it out. But I wrote *Angela's Ashes,* the actual writing, in thirteen months, after having built up to it for thirty years, maybe. Everything converged at the end of that pen—the thirty years of teaching, the oral traditions that I grew up with in Ireland. All of this came together when I wrote the book. And then my own admonitions to my students were ringing in my head: Keep it simple."

Why do you think so many writers have trouble getting a real human tone on the page?

"I think it has a lot to do with education. I think there are people teaching writing who don't know how to write—the professors whose heads are in the academic clouds and who want to be sophisticated and convoluted and they dread simplicity. One of the weaknesses, I think, in the whole educational system is the arrival of young teachers who've just come from undergraduate or graduate studies and they've been listening to professors who've been going on and on about new criticism and modernism and postmodernism and so on, and reading very,

very scholarly books bristling with footnotes and bibliographies. So they arrive in the classroom, the high school classroom, and they don't know how to talk to the kids. And they're competing with television and rock music and everything else. They just don't know how to talk. And it's not their fault. They eschew simplicity."

In your writing, you've toyed with the rules a bit—for instance, not using quotation marks in Angela's Ashes. *What was your thinking behind that decision?*

"With *Angela's Ashes,* I wanted to keep things as simple as possible. I didn't see a child of four using sophisticated punctuation. I think I used commas and periods, and that was it, because I'm terrified of semicolons and maybe colons, too—a child would be, anyway. So I just avoided them. Other writers have done it, too. An Irish friend of mine named Ben Kiely, he would use a dash instead of quotation marks. But I didn't even use a dash at the beginning of the sentence to show that someone was speaking. I just wanted to challenge myself in a very dangerous way. I said to myself: The reader will know who is speaking. It can't be anybody else. I could have put quotation marks in, but I didn't want to because it was a child."

Ian Frazier: "I arrived at it through plenty of trial and error, and it continues. Your voice as an older writer is not the same as your voice as a younger writer at all. So it's not ever finished. I just listen; I constantly listen. Right now I'm really listening for old-guy voices, the white-guy voice, the sort of suburban white-guy voice, which is, in many ways, quite boring (though it might happen, unfortunately, to be your own voice). You hear it in places like in the later Walker Percy books; you can hear an actual guy talking, and that's really how he sounds. Or something like one of the last pieces William F. Buckley wrote that appeared in *The New Yorker*—it's just William F. Buckley talking the way he talks. To me it's just fascinating; I liked the sound of that. John Cheever's journals—they're fascinating to read because you're really hearing Cheever's voice. This is really what he sounded like.

"To me it's a question of listening and listening all the time. And I think you find your voice when you are least aware of it. If you're trying to describe something outside yourself and you're honestly just describing it so somebody else can hear it or see it, you forget about how you want yourself to look, and you look the way you really do look. I also take as an absolute rule for this something that Saul Steinberg told me. Saul was a good friend of mine, and I spent a lot of time with him. I draw—I'm not very good, but I draw—and Saul told me one time that anything that is a drawing of something real is automatically a good drawing. That is, if you're trying without any fanciness to convey something that you see, then it's a good drawing.

"It can happen when you lose yourself in just trying to explain something. I wrote a profile of Heloise that appeared in *The New Yorker* in 1982, and I was asked by an editor to write a paragraph that was just purely descriptive; the editor had said, 'Look, we don't know where you are right here, and we need a paragraph to ground the reader.' So I wrote a paragraph that I thought of as sort of boilerplate—not exactly that, but that it was obligatory and not some fabulous fillip that I wanted to throw in there. At that time *The New Yorker* was running ads in *The New York Times* where they would take a whole page and pick out blocks from different pieces to run in larger type. And that's the paragraph they took. When I read that quote in the ad, I realized that I hadn't seen it as anything special because I was simply trying to make something. I'd had to simply *do* something as opposed to try to be fabulous in some way. It hadn't been part of my scheme; it wasn't like I thought I was getting off a good one. It was just work rather than art, I thought, and yet when you look at it from a distance, you see that work like that is, or can be, art, you know? I just read somewhere where Hemingway said that if you write a story and then take out all the good parts and it's still a story, then you have a story. Sometimes I'll have something saved up, thinking, *Oh, this is a good one, man, this is gonna knock 'em dead,* and then when I put it in it's just apparent that there's no reason for it to be there. It's indulgent, and I end up taking it out."

Dave Barry: "E. B. White sums it up pretty well. I think that my goal when I write is to have the reader pretty much hear what I'm saying in his mind, as if I'm saying it to him. I don't think that everything you write should necessarily be written to be read aloud, but it should sound, in your mind, simple and clear and direct and conversational, unless you're striving deliberately to sound pompous or whatever, which I do sometimes as a humorist. I want the readers to feel as though that's an actual person and that, not only is he writing to them, but he doesn't view himself as their superior. I think if you write naturally and directly, it's a lot like when you talk to people; you know when people are being condescending or pompous, and you don't like it. In speech it's really obvious, but I think people sense it as well in writing, and I always try to make it clear that I'm just trying to tell them what I'm thinking, not trying to blow them away with the immense importance of the thought.

"I went through various stages as a writer. But pretty early on, once I got out of college, and even some while I was in college, because I wrote humor columns for the paper, I came to the conclusion that I was never going to be a towering academic. My writing was best and most appealing to people when it was direct and simple and accessible. I don't ever want readers wondering what I'm thinking.

"At this point, I'm pretty comfortable with getting the voice right on the page. I feel that my technique is pretty solid and I'm comfortable. The hard part for me is *what* to say. That's always been much harder for me than how to say it. I think I'm pretty facile with vocabulary and grammar, and I can get it across if I can figure out what the hell it is. The issue with humor is you don't generally know what it is that you're trying to say. You're really just more trying to get people to laugh and trying to figure out which combination of words will do that, and it's not always connected directly to a thought."

Why do you think so many writers have trouble coming across naturally on the page?

"I think part of it is that they are not taught that that's a good thing. It's funny, because students are told a lot to express themselves. But most of the writing kids are exposed to, especially when they get to college, is writing that's supposed to impress and demonstrate the writer's intellect and superiority. And you see that a lot also in what passes for discourse on the Internet, where there's a tremendous amount of bloviating and sneering and posturing. I don't know when you get a chance to just be clear. When you write in college, your papers generally have to be so many words—I don't know if they still do it that way, but I assume they do—and that always seemed to be more important than what the words actually said. When you think about it, beyond a very early age, it doesn't seem very common for kids to be taught to just express themselves clearly. There's another part of this thing—kids just don't have a lot to say. They're usually writing because they've been told they have to write a thousand words; it's not that they have strong views about whatever the given subject is."

Adam Gopnik: "My first experience of being obsessive about writing was when I was a kid. My parents had a copy of *The Thurber Carnival*, which I read to pieces in bed when I was about seven years old. And the tone of that book, Thurber's tone, appealed to me—more than his humor, more than his stories. It's very different from White's tone. One of the reasons why I admire White so much is that he is an editorialist. He has strong views on things he tries to persuade you of. And Thurber was not that. Thurber was not an opinionated writer in that way. But I loved that tone and I wanted to find a tone like it. I think that more than anything else what you struggle for as a writer is a voice—discovering your voice, finding your voice.

"One of the *New Yorker* writers who helped me enormously in finding my voice was a very obscure one, Maeve Brennan, who wrote beautiful pieces for 'Talk of the Town' under the rubric of the Long-Winded Lady. I came to New York to be an academic, or at least to pretend to be an academic, to study to get my doctorate in art history. I was surrounded by academic prose, and I was writing, for my graduate school work, argumentative, obnoxious academic prose. And finding Maeve Brennan's work in a little bookstore around the corner was a reminder, in extreme form, of the virtues of descriptive writing, the virtues of connecting sentences with *and*, the virtues of simplicity. And I remember trying in those days to write for *The New Yorker*, who of course had no interest in having me write for them, and just writing the simple sentence 'I am a student at the Institute of Fine Arts, and I work part time at the Frick Art Reference Library' and suddenly feeling a kind of click: *Oh yes, that's the way to write. If I follow that line of simple, almost faux-naïf declarative statements, I'll get somewhere.* And that, in fact, became the first sentence of the first piece I ever had in *The New Yorker.* I think that, more than anything else, voice is what we search for as writers, and whenever I go right, it's because I remember that discovery; I remember the virtues of soulfulness and simplicity. And whenever I go wrong, it's when I fall back into the academic role and I resort to punchiness and polemic."

At this point does your voice come naturally to you, or is there still a lot of toil involved?

"There's still endless toil involved, but the voice does come more naturally. You recognize it more readily when you've got it. My friend Louis Menand said beautifully once that when he starts writing, he struggles, but that there's a little kind of daemon or puppet inside him named Luke—Louis's nickname is Luke—and Luke starts writing and then everything is okay. To me it's like when you're riding a stationary bike and you're huffing and puffing and your lungs are working hard, and then suddenly it kind of clicks in. My literary aerobics click in, and it sounds like me on the page, which is nothing at all like what I sound like in person. My wife laughs about this all the time. People have an impression that they'll find a kind of wise and serene guy at the other end of that type of prose, and I'm neither of those things."

At the other end of the style spectrum, do you spend a lot of time fussing over the smaller elements of mechanics, punctuation, and grammar?

"I do, but I will shamefacedly admit that I have come over these years to rely so much on Ann Goldstein [head of *The New Yorker*'s copy department] that I will often defer solving a problem that I know is a problem, and just say to Ann, who has not only absolute knowledge but perfect pitch in these things, 'You do it.' Because I know whatever she does will be right. We disagree about a few things time and again, but they're usually questions of rhythm. You know, good writing depends so much on rhythm, and one of the things that *The Elements of Style* won't give you is a sense of rhythm. It's like when you're learning to play an instrument; you can learn which keys to press, but you have to internalize rhythm. And rhythm and phrasing are as important, in the long run, as hitting the right notes. So we tear our hair out a lot about rhythm and phrasing, but I have such blind faith in Ann's knowledge that I probably defer to her more than I should. I *know* I defer more to her than I should, because when I have books to do, I'm often helpless without her. It's funny, I just finished reading *The Art of Burning Bridges: A Life of John O'Hara*, by Geoffrey Wolff. And O'Hara was driven crazy by that kind of *New Yorker* punctiliousness and fussing, because he depended entirely on rhythm and phrasing to do what he was trying to do. But I love it. I feel married to *New Yorker* style. But it's like my marriage to my wife. It's a choice I've made rather than an edict given. Let me rephrase that: It was a choice *she* made rather than an edict given."

Will Blythe: "One of the things Strunk and White say, and that I agree with, is to try to use the paragraph as your basic unit of composition. That's a great idea. But to construct an interesting paragraph, you might as well try to write a symphony. You're trying to use rhythm and speed and pauses to create this thing that makes sense in terms of sound as much as meaning. So in some ways, I'm going for that musical element in the composition of a paragraph, and then as a by-product of that I end up, I hope, with some kind of clarity and some kind of precision. It's a by-product of this thing that is much harder to articulate, because it's nonverbal; it's a musical quality that I hope the prose has. I guess it's voice, really. The ideas almost come from the music of the sentence. Sometimes when I'm writing a sentence, I'll put 'something, something TK (to come), and something TK'—so that I'm setting up a musical structure that I'm then going to fill in with meaning. And if the meaning contradicts something that I've said before, I might well go back and rewrite the thing I said earlier, so that I can get to that sentence that I love. There's a book by Richard Hugo called *The Triggering Town,* in which he makes a distinction that I didn't understand at the time, and maybe I do now—a distinction between music and truth. He talks about two kinds of poets, those who go for music first and those who go for truth first.

"When I write a review or an essay, the thing that really gets me into it is trying to create this object made of sentences, and I want the sentences to be interesting. I'm writing about whatever the subject is, but in the meantime I'm also trying to make a little bit of music. I hope that doesn't sound pretentious. It's just that my means of composition has as much to do with sound as it does to do with sense. So that clarity, weirdly enough in that case, is almost like an accidental by-product of this attempt to make something that has a musical sort of structure, a voice. I'm trying to get to a certain kind of meaning that is produced as much through the rhythm of the sentence, and through the stops and the breaks and the places where I go long and places where I go short, as through the actual argument."

Does your process of finding your voice work in the way that White says it does in his Chapter V essay?

"At the end, I come out with something—I attempt it anyway—that has those virtues that White talks about. And I have come to recognize something; it's an E. B. White realization, and it goes back to what he said about placing yourself in the background. When I was a younger writer, I used to strive much harder for effect. I felt like, *I've gotta make an impression in this sentence.* I think I wrote prose that was much louder and more assertive than it needed to be. I don't go back and reread much of my old stuff because it makes me cringe. But now, in my gray wisdom, I realize that whatever you are is going to come out in your writing; you don't have to strive that hard. I think if you've been doing it for enough years, you don't have to strive to be loud or to make an impression because whatever you are is going to be sufficiently there. That's caused me to relax a lot as a writer and not strive so much to constantly make all my sentences interesting—and I know this sounds contradictory to what I said earlier about my focus on the sentence—but some sentences are right if they're not interesting, they're just bridge sentences. But placing yourself in the background, I think there's great truth to that that I would not have understood, really, when I was twenty."

Damon Lindelof: "My process is a multidraft process, and by the time the piece ends up getting published—whether it's an essay I write that just goes out on the Internet or, for example, some of the pieces I wrote during the television writers' strike, or an op-ed in *The New York Times*—what people end up reading is usually about the seventh or eighth draft of the piece. Part of my writing process is finding what voice I want to be speaking in. The tone, for me, is always the most challenging part. I tend to usually begin with something that is tongue-in-cheek, sarcastic, hiding behind sort of attempted wit, as opposed to a drive toward sincerity, because sincerity is, at times, a lot more difficult to write and, more importantly, a lot harder to access in yourself. But as I move on, especially if I'm letting the right people read it and give me notes—such as an editor or my wife (who is probably my best editor) sort of cracking the whip and telling me when I'm really hiding or trying to be clever and pithy as opposed to being honest—then, as a result of that, usually my true voice can emerge without being overly sentimental or, on the other side, too cute for its own good. I don't think I have the self-discipline at this point in my career to find it on my own. My process is extremely collaborative. It requires bouncing ideas off people and engaging in conversations with my peers in order to arrive at something that's even halfway decent."

8

An Audience of One

Soulwise, these are trying times.
—E. B. WHITE

William Strunk Jr. *retired* from Cornell University in 1937, forty-six years after first arriving on the campus. Shortly after, he and Emilie moved to Princeton, New Jersey, to be near their son Oliver, who had just taken up his post in musicology at Princeton University. At least a portion of Strunk's time in retirement was spent helping his son with translations of primary texts on music history. Oliver put his father to work translating from Latin, French, German, and Italian. Will Strunk Jr.'s translations are still credited in the latest edition of Oliver Strunk's *Source Readings in Music History*, which remains a standard work in the field, now updated by a new general editor (Oliver died in 1980).

By the summer of 1942, William and Emilie had returned to Ithaca. Strunk enjoyed keeping up with goings-on on campus and socializing with the friends he had made among the Cornell faculty and alumni. At the end of 1943, he was called out of retirement—briefly, as it happened—and he wrote to tell E. B. White about the experience:

January 26/44

Dear Andy:

I read with interest your account of being deturbinated and acting as a nurse's aide (or is it aid?). Congratulations on your now having a sound nose in a sound body.

During the last two months of last year I had an experience like that of "on again, gone again, Finnegan." I was called in to relieve the manpower shortage in the English Department, and began teaching civilian freshman English (about three-fourths girls). It was very interesting and gave me a feeling like that of a returned exile. But after three weeks I had to take two weeks off when I caught pneumonitis and after another week, I ran into a cold wave and had a chill and then a fever and went back to bed again for a day, and my doctor said I must give up trying to teach in the Ithaca winter. The trouble seemed to lie in waiting on corners for buses in temperatures below freezing, sometimes considerably below. So I sadly acquiesced and telephoned in my resignation. Now I don't go up on the campus unless I like the weather. . . .

Please present my best compliments to Mrs. White. All best regards to you.

As ever,
W. S. Jr.

Throughout his retirement years, Strunk maintained a continuing correspondence with E. B. White. Strunk had been a *New Yorker* subscriber since 1934 and kept up with everything White published, both in that magazine and in *Harper's* (in a letter thanking White for a gift copy of *One Man's Meat*, Strunk wrote that he had followed the *Harper's* column faithfully, welcoming each new installment "like a monthly letter"). In the last decades of his life, in long, genial letters to White, written in the expansive mode of a professor emeritus with time on his hands, Strunk passed on English Department news and campus gossip ("The 'Cornell Daily Sun,' for which you . . . once wrote, is now appearing in a weekly issue called the 'Bulletin,' and is in very low estate. . . . It is full of misprimts and the speling and grammer is not very good. Apparently the subscribers are satisfied"); he praised articles he had enjoyed in *The New Yorker;* he suggested potential "Notes and Comment" topics to White and story ideas that other *New Yorker* writers might wish to pursue; he pointed out mistakes of fact he had found in the magazine as well as infelicities of style ("Between ourselves, [Janet Flanner's] metaphor about Pétain in 1870, 'headed, like an old shoe, for retirement and a pension,' seems to need blocking. Or, if 'headed' hardly rates as a metaphor, then the simile needs revamping"); he pointed out solecisms he'd spotted elsewhere, perhaps with the thought that White could use them as fodder for newsbreaks, the little column-ending fillers in which *The New Yorker* poked wry fun at mistakes printed in other periodicals and newspapers ("I observe that today's *New York Times,* in telling about a new version of the Bible, says that the King James Version is based on the Latin Vulgate. I expect that they will get not a few letters setting them straight"); he critiqued *New Yorker* cover art; he talked about writing and writers he enjoyed (he admired White's good friend James Thurber and fellow *New Yorker* writers Frank Sullivan and Russell Maloney, and he was "greatly taken" with the work of Vladimir Nabokov).

A reader wrote to complain about an error in an early printing of the third edition.

Dear Mr. _____

    Thanks for your card. I'm as sad as you are. My eyes are not good enough for proofreading any more, but I always hope somebody in the publishing house can still see.

                    Sincerely,
                    E. B. White

In the spring of 1940, E. B. White sought Strunk's suggestions for authors and works to include in the humor anthology that White and his wife, Katharine, were then compiling and that was published in 1941, *A Subtreasury of American Humor.* Strunk was pleased to have been asked and on the book's publication wrote a review for the *Cornell Alumni News.* He enjoyed the *Subtreasury;* three years after the anthology was published, he was still talking about it:

February 8/44

Dear Andy:

    I am glad to learn that the impostures of Matthias have a chance of being retold in THE NEW YORKER. Thank you for your efforts in the cause.

    For a long time I have resisted the impulse, but now yield to it, to give you the list of my five favorites in the "Subtreasury of American Humor." Arranged alphabetically by authors, they are:

The Party Over There
The Latest Improvements in Artillery
Inflexible Logic
Old Families, Move Over
Dusk in Fierce Pajamas

I should like to be able to award five gold Oscars (two of them posthumously) to the authors and not mind the expense.

Some time next month I may get down to New York for a few days, but it is still a bit uncertain. If I do I shall count on seeing you.

> *Best regards, as ever,*
> *Will*

Letters from Strunk continued to reach White, at *The New Yorker* and on the farm in Maine, through the fall of 1945, less than a year before Strunk's death. In what may have been his last letter to White, Strunk praised White's first book for children, *Stuart Little*, which had just been published, and he offered to return the old papers saved from White's days in the Manuscript Club. He also let White know that *The New Yorker* had recently made a mistake in a passing reference to the "hanging" of John Wilkes Booth. "I was surprised," he wrote, "to find no comment under the head of 'Department of Amplification and Correction.'"

The next news E. B. White received about his old friend came in April 1946 from Strunk's only daughter, Dr. Catherine Amatruda.

Dear Andy,

For so I remember you, and so my father always spoke of you (I am William Strunk's daughter).

I am writing to tell you the unhappy news about my father. In

the past week or two he suffered a serious mental breakdown. He
became so ill that hospital care was advised. Because he could not
appreciate his own condition court commitment to a hospital for
the mentally ill was necessary. The sad fact is that he was admitted
to the Willard State Hospital, last Wednesday.

I have visited and we feel reassured that everything possible
will be done for him. He is doing as well as can be expected; we can
only hope for the best.

He spoke of you so often, I felt you would want to know.

Most sincerely,
Catherine S. Amatruda

Strunk was being treated for "senile psychosis," an organic, age-
related dementia, at Willard State Hospital in Willard, New York,
near Seneca Lake, one Finger Lake over from Cayuga and about
thirty miles northwest of Ithaca. E. B. White's reply to Catherine
no longer survives, but it's apparent that he asked about the possibility of writing to Strunk. Catherine answered.

Dear Andy,

Thank you for your very nice letter. It is good of you to suggest
writing to father. He has finally written one or two letters home
and has asked specifically that we not forward mail to him and
asked not to be given news of people outside the family. On a
recent visit he told my brother that he feared bad news on opening
letters and preferred not to receive them. In time he may change in
this feeling, but now we are following his wishes very carefully.

He is about to be moved to the Westchester Branch of the New
York Hospital, where we hope he will be more comfortable and
where we can visit him more readily. My mother is moving down
to New Haven, so we will all be close together.

We are, of course, heart broken over all this but he does seem
a little better and actually writes that he is trying to worry less
and to share & sympathize with his fellow patients! I thought it
wonderful.

Your tribute to him touched me very much.

> *Sincerely,*
> *Catherine Amatruda*

The planned move to Westchester seems not to have taken
place. Instead, in late June, after a two-month stay at Willard,
Strunk was transferred to the Hudson River Psychiatric Institute
in Poughkeepsie, New York, where he lived out the remaining
three months of his life and died of general arteriosclerosis on
the morning of September 26, 1946. He was seventy-seven years
old. Funeral services were held in Sage Chapel on the Cornell
campus, and he was buried in a family plot in Pleasant Grove
Cemetery, just north of the university. Strunk was memorialized
in Cornell's *Necrology of the Faculty*:

Attracted to the study of letters by his innate love of the word
and of creative thought, he gave his life to the communication
of beauty and wisdom. Disdaining specialization, he ranged over
many fields of knowledge. He began as a teacher of mathematics;
he was at home in the classic and foreign literatures and cultures.
Though his scholarship was exact and extensive, though his ef-
fervescent curiosity led him into endless explorations of curious
and knotty problems, he maintained in word and practice that
the end of the literary scholar is not to solve problems but to
lighten the environing darkness. . . . Professor Strunk was for a
good half century on this campus an exemplar of the humane
scholarly life. The benign quality of his mind showed forth in

all his dealings. When his old students and his old companions gather, their talk is all of his kindness, his helpfulness as teacher and colleague, his boyish lack of envy and guile.

Strunk's death occurred as White's career was in full stride. The professor had lived long enough to enjoy twenty years of his star student's career in letters, to see White lauded as one of America's premier essayists, and, with the publication of *Stuart Little,* to witness the beginning of his career as a celebrated children's author. But Strunk missed the entire back half of White's literary output, from *Charlotte's Web* and *The Trumpet of the Swan* to *Letters of E. B. White* and the rebirth of *The Elements of Style;* White's multiple honorary degrees; and his many awards, including the Presidential Medal of Freedom, the National Medal for Literature, and the Pulitzer Prize.

E. B. White gave up writing "Notes and Comment" on a regular basis in 1955, but he continued to contribute pieces to *The New Yorker,* including his "Letters from the East" and newsbreak taglines, for many years to come. After Katharine's death in 1977, he stayed on the farm, working and writing, and answering the many fan letters that continued to fill his mailbox, until his own health began to deteriorate. His weekly work on newsbreaks came to an end in 1982, when his failing eyesight had begun to make reading and writing difficult. He wrote a note of regret to the *New Yorker* editor William Shawn, thanking him and the magazine "for keeping me gainfully employed over such a long period of time." In addition to his bad eyesight, White also suffered from a heart blockage, poor hearing, and arthritis, which made typing difficult. In "Andy," a remembrance of E. B. White published in *The New Yorker* in 2005, his stepson, Roger Angell, wrote that, in August 1984, White had banged his head while removing a canoe from atop his car, and that he took to his bed a couple months after that "and never again knew exactly where he was." The doctors' initial diagnosis was Alzheimer's, but they eventually decided that White was, instead, suffering from senile dementia. Nurses were brought in to care for him. Though he had some trouble communicating in the last months of his life, he enjoyed being read to by his son, Joel, and he never lost his ability to recognize his friends and family members. E. B. White died at home on October 1, 1985. His ashes are interred beside those of Katharine in the Brooklin Cemetery.

ROGER ANGELL

I'm not absolutely certain about why *The Elements of Style* has been so popular, but I've always been drawn to it because of its simplicity and clarity. It takes up the universally dreaded difficulty of writing well in an informal, everyday manner. There is a useful table of contents. There are numbered sections and subsections, set off in boldface type, and countless examples. It makes you feel as if learning to write well is a process, like assembling a tricycle: something that anyone can do in time. Most of all, its central precepts are easy to remember and really do help: "Write in a way that comes naturally." . . . "Revise and rewrite." . . . "Do not explain too much." . . . "Avoid fancy words." . . . "Be clear."

E. B. White's *The Elements of Style* is a good book because it follows its own advice. Or so it seems to me.

Roger Angell, stepson of E. B. White, has been an editor and writer for *The New Yorker* for more than fifty years. He is the author of many books; his latest is *Let Me Finish*.

The New Yorker responded to the passing of this most influential element of its own style by dedicating the "Notes and Comment" section of the October 14, 1985, issue to remembrances of E. B. White. The tribute included contributions from the editor William Shawn and the writers John Updike and Roger Angell. Shawn credited White for having developed "a new literary form: brief personal essays, conversational, lyrical, idiosyncratic, yet somehow capable of striking some chord common to all of us." Shawn said White had served as a model writer "not only at *The New Yorker* but for many, if not most, of our country's writers. Other writers took their bearings from him, and learned from him a respect for craft and discipline and language."

Dear Mr. White,

   I'm omitting needless words!

                    Sincerely yours,
                    [a reader]

Dear Ms. _____

   Thanks. So am I.

                    Yrs,
                    E. B. White

The outpouring from the broader press was swift and heartfelt. The nation's journalists, many of whom had likely learned their craft with the help of *The Elements of Style* and had been drawn to their careers by E. B. White's inspiration, felt the significance of the occasion and reached for a measure of White-like eloquence in the summing up. "White's death may have been the most melancholy event of the year for anyone who cares about the quality of prose and about neatness, aptness and originality of thought," wrote Charles Champlin in the *Los Angeles Times*. "He celebrated, with eloquent simplicity, the pleasure of doing the tangible chores (the primary and the near) that derive from the larger and abstract gifts under which we live." Herbert Mitgang, in *The New York Times*, praised White as a "great essayist, a supreme stylist. His literary style was as pure as any in our language. It was singular, colloquial, clear, unforced, thoroughly American and utterly beautiful. Because of his quiet influence, several generations of this country's writers write better than they might have done. He never wrote a mean or careless sentence." Leslie Hanscom, writing in *Newsday*, admitted the daunting nature of the task at hand: "To try to write about [White] is a nervous and self-conscious act, because he is part of the conscience with which one writes."

Hanscom was half right. For those writers who know and care, White (with Strunk, with *Elements*) remains a living presence in the conscience. But it's nothing to be nervous about. White would have repudiated—did, in fact, repudiate—the notion that he, or Strunk, or *The Elements of Style*, should loom, cloudlike, over writers who, after all, are only trying to get their work done. As White himself wrote, in the book's closing paragraphs, "The whole duty of a writer is to please and satisfy himself, and the true writer always plays to an audience of one." Neither author is watching over us, and style isn't something we gain by trying our hardest to write like E. B. White. White took pains to be clear on the point: Style is not achieved by proxy, nor is it an add-on, something you find elsewhere and bring home to spread atop your writing like a meringue. Style is *you*.

For those writers who know and care, *The Elements of Style* lives lightly in the conscience. Strunk and White are companionable spirits, good company for writers or, as it happens, just about anyone else. Their book is less a mandate than a gathering of hints and assurances about a small number of big truths that we sometimes forget—truths that may have been leached from us by careless teachers or obscured by the hard news of the day or even shamed out of us by our own flaws and failures. *The Elements of Style* invites us to remember that we can trust in our ability to think things through and set our thoughts down straight and clear; that with a little effort we can hope to sight a line of order in the chaos; that things will improve as we simplify our purposes and speak our minds; and that we must believe, as E. B. White put it, "in the truth and worth of the scrawl."

ACKNOWLEDGMENTS

Late in 1958, when he was hip-deep in the remodeling of Will Strunk's little book, E. B. White wrote to his editor, Jack Case, "I feel a terrible responsibility in this project, and it is making me jumpy." I know the feeling. I don't know that a writer can risk calling down any more trouble on his own head than by taking for his subject America's most famous writing guide and one of our best writers. I wouldn't have attempted it without the help and encouragement of many good people. I want to acknowledge them here, and not spare the modifiers.

A sincere *thank-you* to Michelle Howry, my editor, for this opportunity and for your skillful work—what a treat to meet up again; Michael Bourret, of Dystel & Goderich Literary Management, for your help and your helpful ear; Allene White and Martha White, daughter-in-law and granddaughter of E. B. White, for your overwhelming generosity; Susan Beach, grandniece of William Strunk Jr., and Will Amatruda, Will Jr.'s grandson, for your enthusiasm, indispensable help, and patience with my many questions; Alec Wilkinson, for your kind help from the beginning—if not for you, this book would not have happened; Adam Gopnik, for your early interest and a delightful conversation that helped this book find a home; all the other writers who generously shared their time and thoughts—Roger Angell, Nicholson Baker, Dave Barry, Roy Blount Jr., Will Blythe, Ian

Frazier, Thomas Kunkel, Elmore Leonard, Damon Lindelof, Frank McCourt, and Sharon Olds; Joseph Opiela and Susan Aspey of Longman, publishers of *The Elements of Style,* for your interest and your help; Susan M. S. Brown, copy editor, for your sharp ear and careful eye; Steve Sullivan, for encouragement, useful facts, and your friendship; Karen Altstadt, my sister, for speedy transcriptions and steadfast cheerleading; Don Prues, for helpful chats, friendship, and passwords; Theresa Bengel, for your help with the early research; Ana Guimaraes and the staff at Cornell University Library's Rare and Manuscript Collections, for your cheerful and knowledgeable assistance; Richard Hunt, for solitude, reasonably priced.

Among the teachers who contributed their time and expertise, I want to particularly thank Dr. Michael Carson, Terrence Cheeseman, Dr. Russel Durst, Dr. Keith Hjortshoj, and Dr. Lucille Schultz. All have long experience working with young writers, and our conversations were invaluable.

Thank you to my son, Sam Garvey, and my daughter, Sarah Garvey; you both inspire and help in more ways than you know. Finally, to Deb Garvey, my wife of twenty-eight years: Thank you for your edits, your patience, your faith, and your love.

BIBLIOGRAPHY

Anderson, Bruce. "Professor Strunk and Mr. White's Little Book." *Cornell Magazine* 98, no. 9 (1996): 25–31.

Aristotle. *The Art of Rhetoric.* Trans. H. C. Lawson-Tancred. New York: Penguin Group (USA), 1991.

Aristotle. *Rhetoric.* Trans. W. Rhys Roberts. Mineola, N.Y.: Dover Publications, 2004.

Bogel, Fredric V., and Katherine K. Gottschalk, eds. *Teaching Prose: A Guide for Writing Instructors.* New York: W. W. Norton & Company, 1988.

Brereton, John C., ed. *The Origins of Composition Studies in the American College, 1875–1925: A Documentary History.* Pittsburgh: University of Pittsburgh Press, 1995.

E. B. White collection, #4619. Division of Rare and Manuscript Collections, Cornell University Library.

Elledge, Scott. *E. B. White: A Biography.* New York: W. W. Norton & Company, 1984.

Fried, Debra. "Bewhiskered Examples in *The Elements of Style.*" *Western Humanities Review* 45, no. 4 (1991): 304–311.

Kane, Robert H. *Quest for Meaning: Values, Ethics, and the Modern Experience.* Chantilly, Va.: The Teaching Company. Compact disc.

Kunkel, Thomas. *Genius in Disguise: Harold Ross of* The New Yorker. New York: Carroll & Graf Publishers, 1996.

Lang, Berel. "Strunk and White and Grammar as Morality." *Soundings: An Interdisciplinary Journal* 65, no. 1 (1982): 23–30.

Letters of E. B. White. Originally edited by Dorothy Lobrano Guth and revised and updated by Martha White. New York: HarperCollins Publishers, 2006.

Lundgren, Jodi. "Interrogating the Popularity of Strunk and White." *Journal of Teaching Writing* 18, nos. 1–2 (2000): 123–32.

McCaughey, G. S. "A Multi-Million Dollar Hoax?" *Humanities Association Bulletin* 15, no. 1 (1964): 31–37.

Minear, Richard H. "E. B. White Takes His Leave, or Does He? The Elements of Style, Six Editions (1918–2000)." *The Massachusetts Review* 45, no. 1 (2004): 51–77.

Pullum, Geoffrey K. *Automated Adverb Hunting and Why You Don't Need It.* Language Log. http://itre.cis.upenn.edu/~myl/languagelog/archives/004271.html.

———. "Ideology, Power, and Linguistic Theory." Paper presented in a special session at the 2004 Convention of the Modern Language Association, Philadelphia, Penn., December 2004.

———. *Those Who Take the Adjectives from the Table.* Language Log. http://itre.cis.upenn.edu/~myl/languagelog/archives/000469.html.

Reynolds, Nedra, Patricia Bizzell, and Bruce Herzberg. *The Bedford Bibliography for Teachers of Writing.* Boston: Bedford/St. Martin's, 2003.

Root, Robert L. Jr. *E. B. White: The Emergence of an Essayist.* Iowa City: University of Iowa Press, 1999.

Strunk, William Jr. *The Elements of Style.* Ithaca, N.Y.: Privately printed, 1918.

Strunk, William Jr., and E. B. White. *The Elements of Style.* New York: Macmillan Publishing, 1959.

———. *The Elements of Style.* 2nd ed. New York: Macmillan Publishing, 1972.

———. *The Elements of Style.* 3rd ed. New York: Macmillan Publishing, 1979.

———. *The Elements of Style.* 4th ed., revised. White Plains, N.Y.: Longman Publishing Group, 1999.

White, E. B. *Essays of E. B. White.* New York: HarperCollins Publishers, 1977.

———. *One Man's Meat.* New York: Harper & Row, Publishers, 1944.

———. *Writings from* The New Yorker, *1927–1976.* Ed. Rebecca M. Dale. New York: HarperCollins Publishers, 1990.

Worby, Diana Zacharia. "In Search of a Common Language: Women and Educational Texts." *College English* 41, no. 1 (1979): 101–105.

Yagoda, Ben. *About Town: The* New Yorker *and the World It Made.* Cambridge, Mass.: Da Capo Press, 2000.

mL

11/09